Expressive Movement

*Posture and Action in Daily Life,
Sports, and the Performing Arts*

Alexandra Pierce, Ph.D.
and
Roger Pierce, Ph.D.

INSIGHT BOOKS

PLENUM PRESS • NEW YORK AND LONDON

Library of Congress Cataloging in Publication Data

Pierce, Alexandra.
  Expressive movement: posture and action in daily life, sports, and the performing
arts / Alexandra and Roger Pierce.
      p.   cm.
  Includes index.
  ISBN 0-306-43269-2
  1. Movement therapy. 2. Movement, Psychology of. I. Pierce, Roger. II. Title.
RC489.M66P54   1989   88-13600
615.8′2—dc19   CIP

The translations of material from the *Duino Elegies* by Rainer Maria Rilke, appearing
on pages 119, 192, and 218, were done by Drs. Alexandra and Roger Pierce
by permission of Insel-Verlag, and W. W. Norton and Company, Inc., New York,
New York

Drawings and tracings by Roger Pierce.

© 1989 Alexandra Pierce and Roger Pierce
Plenum Press is a Division of Plenum Publishing Corporation
233 Spring Street, New York, N.Y. 10013

Printed in the United States of America

To

Ida Rolf
Heinrich Schenker
Franz Schubert

Preface

Because the education of movement transforms the whole person, it embraces the ethics and aesthetics as well as the mechanics of activity.

This book is designed to meet a broad spectrum of readers, from those who are looking over the field with intellectual detachment to those who wish to guide themselves through a shift in their habitual movement patterns.

We have often resorted to narrative in order to keep the experiential nature of this work apparent and to suggest the possibility for personal application. The characters, including Thomas the teacher, are fictional; their stories have been knitted from our encounters in movement teaching.

Alexandra Pierce and Roger Pierce

Redlands, California

Acknowledgments

Anyone familiar with the work of Ida Rolf will recognize our debt to her. She was a committed teacher and for us one of those forces that turns life strongly in a particular direction; she speaks for herself eloquently in her writings. Others who have strongly influenced us, either directly or through their writings or intermediaries, are Heinrich Schenker, Judith Aston, F. M. Alexander, and Charlotte Selver.

We are grateful to our son, Benjamin Pierce, for the richness of his contribution to our thinking and writing, and to our daughter, Jessica Pierce, for the suggestiveness of her research into reverence for nature.

A. P.
R. P.

Contents

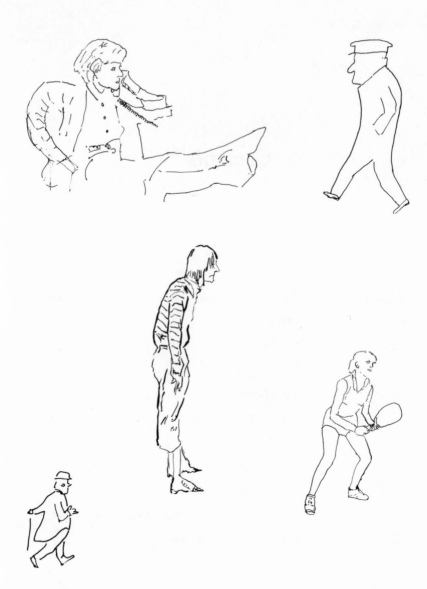

Character, attitude, and values are often immediately evident in the carriage of the body.

Chapter 1

Movement Expresses Values

We strive all the time to give our life its form, but we do
so by copying willy-nilly, like a drawing, the features of
the person we are and not of the person we should like
to be.
  Marcel Proust, *Remembrance of Things Past*
  (1913–1927) 1981, II: 191–192

Movement as Aesthetic Action

You are reading these words with your body—not just your
eyes and your brain, but your whole body. The angle of your
head, the depth of your breathing, the tension level of the
muscles along your spine and around your mouth are parts of
a pattern that is at this moment expressing your attitude and
your response as you read. These so-called physical factors

are not separate from your alertness, your receptivity, your capacity to focus, your sense of humor—the whole rich un-differentiated realm that you call "reading."

We humans take pride in being able to shape ourselves and our destinies, presumably in the light of a basic form which we sense to be true of ourselves. Yet we are sur-prisingly careless about examining what this innate form ac-tually is; a cursory scan around a roomful of people yields sufficient evidence that we often mold ourselves into shapes that violate our nature. Looking at ourselves from the per-spective of movement—of action in the most down-to-earth sense—provides a simple and accessible opportunity to ponder our natural form and then true our behavior to it so that we more accurately express who we are.

In one sense this opportunity calls for an aesthetic ap-proach to ordinary actions that we don't think of as artistic—walking and sitting, driving the car, taking out the garbage—and for seeing that we do constantly what dancers, musi-cians, and painters do: we make a track through space and time. A pianist, by means of the instrument, translates press-ing or flicking movements of the hands into sound. A painter may make very similar movements and, by stroking a brush full of paint against canvas, translate them into a picture. Everyone is an artist in this sense, and we are capable of shaping our tracks so that they progressively become more eloquent and effective.

You can see in others, perhaps more easily than in your-self, how persuasively the body's movements speak the per-son. Watch ten joggers pass by the front of your house and you will see ten different etchings of individuality: Linda pulls up her shoulders so that her arm movements fight her forward propulsion, as if telling us how difficult all this is and working to ensure the truth of the observation; Michael's feet hit the ground with crashes of impact; Larry floats along as if the ground hardly exists for him.

All human movement is expressive. Sometimes it expresses intention: Jim reaches out and turns the knob because he means to open the door. But he doesn't really intend to tighten his jaw when the boss is rude to him and the waitress spills his coffee and his wife is late. Linda, jogging by with elevated shoulders, does not intend to get in the way of her own running, but she does express a complex layering of personal dynamics in her movement style. And it is a style. She will use this same balance—or imbalance—of muscular forces whether she is jogging, talking on the telephone, cooking dinner, or driving. Her husband and her dog recognize the sound of her footsteps in the hallway upstairs because her movement pattern sets up a recognizable rhythm of sound and vibration in the house.

This personal pattern of movement is one aspect of her character, the present manifestation of all the choices she has made or that have been imposed upon her in the past. The Greek verb *kharassein*, from which our word character is derived, means to scratch or engrave, that is, to make a distinctive mark on something. Life is a process of becoming more and more characterized. We become "characters" as we acquire a history, and that history lives in our present behavior. We are likely to have a strong attitude, positive or negative, toward our own set of characteristics; after all, we have invested in them, have sacrificed many possibilities to hew a pathway through the jungle of options. And yet many of these protected patterns of behavior, grooved in by repetition, were at first picked up randomly and unconsciously. A young child may learn to stand and walk by imitation of—or by resistance to—people who themselves have never given their own walking and standing a moment's thought, whose learning was itself by unconscious modeling.

Woven into the tapestry of a person's characterizing traits are certain patterns that channel emotional energy into behavior which in part represses itself. Seen from a physical perspective, this repressive behavior is a self-defeating habit of excessive muscular contraction—what goes by the name of "tension": one muscle group acts not to produce movement but to inhibit another group. In the old Charles Atlas advertisements for a mail-order muscle-building program, the beach bully kicks sand in the face of the 97-pound weakling while the little man's erstwhile girlfriend looks on scornfully. Caught between anger and fear, the weakling is frozen into immobility; his impulse to strike out is exactly countered by his restraint. He does not move but inwardly is full of sound and fury. His energy, though excited, cancels itself out.

Tension expresses itself not only in people who are "wired" but in those who give the appearance of being slack. Muscular contraction pulls the body off its central axis of support, and then its weight sags down, resting on organs and at the same time calling on the muscular system for an increasingly taut role in holding up the off-balance weight.

Building a Character

Janie, a 5-year-old swept along in the impending divorce of her parents, learns by watching her mother that the appropriate response to someone who doesn't act the way he is "supposed to" is resentment, emerging in a stream of indirect nastiness: cynical comments, burned potatoes, a headache on the morning of a fishing trip. Frustration is demonstrated to Janie as a way of life, and being at the bottom of the pecking order, she is even frustrated in following her mother's example of frustration because she is often punished for it. Trying to influence her parents, she sulks; like the 97-pound weakling, she shows her feelings indirectly to avoid punishment. Deliberately, though somewhat unconsciously, she fashions a style of expression which keeps the emotion simmering. All this takes a sustained commitment of muscular energy.

Janie's older brother Gerald, picking up a character strand from his third-grade teacher, buries his anxiety, grief, and anger under a mask of exaggerated politeness, but his behavior is unctuous and self-seeking, as negative in its way as his mother's barbed cynicism and his sister's nursed resentment. Both children, forgetting their birthright of spontaneity, learn from their social environment to adapt its models to their particular needs and talents; they divert emotional expression into inauthentic, manipulative channels which become habitual.

Their bodies, resonators of the life in them, lose presentness and transparency as they become perpetuators of past experience. The children assume postures. Their social strategies are carried out in their bodies by a steady muscular contraction summoned specifically for the expression: Gerald thrusts his head forward solicitously and pastes on a smile that masks his anxious arrogance. Janie's sulking tightens her rib cage and restricts her breathing, and the consequent reduction of vitality becomes part of her style. She will feel happier from time to time and mostly throw off this pattern, but it leaves a trace on all her behavior, and the more she practices, the more strongly the pattern becomes part of her life, coloring everything she does as she increasingly identifies with it.

Janie's mother, vaguely disturbed by the slack image Janie projects, calls it "slumping." But Janie is hard at work, in ways mostly hidden to herself as well as to her mother, pulling herself off balance and then paying the price, year after year, in the muscular contraction necessary to keep herself upright without the full support of her skeleton.

Character in general, and habitual tension patterns in particular, are the expression of commitment—of caring and values. "Where your treasure is, there will your heart be also." What you love and hate determines the direction of your choosing and striving, that is, your behavior; and conversely, your behavior expresses the nature of your "heart," your pattern of tendencies, compulsions, preferences.

Movement education is often thought to be, and sometimes is, one more set of stock responses to learn, one more whittling off of our individual edges, another starched shirt with a tight collar, designed to encroach on our already limited personal freedoms. But it can take another direction, toward loosening the hold of habit and letting one's light shine among men, fulfilling unexplored potentialities and finding release from joyless and unproductive repetition that hides our humanness under a bushel basket.

Note on Wilhelm Reich

Psychologist Wilhelm Reich found the genesis of character structure in sexual frustration which he thought to be inherent in the family experience of early childhood. He recognized that character was expressed by the musculature and referred to it as armor.

> A conflict which has been active at a certain period of life always leaves its traces in the character, in the form of a rigidity. It functions automatically and is difficult to

eliminate. The patient does not feel it as something alien to him, but often feels it as something rigid and unyielding or as a loss or diminution of spontaneity. Each of these layers in the character structure is a piece of life history which is preserved *in another form* and is still active. . . . If the layers were particularly numerous and functioning automatically, if they formed a compact unit which was difficult to penetrate, they seemed like an *"armor"* surrounding the living organism. This armor may be superficial or deep-lying, soft as a sponge or hard as nails. In each case its function was to protect against unpleasure. However, the organism paid for this protection by losing a great deal of its capacity for pleasure. (Reich 1942, 121–122)

Leaving aside Reich's emphasis on the sexual genesis of armor, his insight into the physical nature of charged frustration is accurate and suggestive. Armor is a fabric of hardened and thickened connective tissue woven through the locomotor structure of the body, and its effect is to establish a set of limitations.

Chapter 2

Depth

who were so dark of heart they might not speak,
a little innocence will make them sing. . . .
        e. e. cummings 1954, 456

What is man but a mass of thawing clay? The ball of the
human finger is but a drop congealed. The fingers and
toes flow to their extent from the thawing mass of the
body. Who knows what the human body would expand
and flow out to under a more genial heaven?
        Henry David Thoreau, *Walden* (1854) 1962, 331–332

The Hierarchy of Structural Levels

For many people the wish that their life were different takes
the form "I wish it were deeper, more meaningful." They
might be thinking of someone with self-discernment, who ful-
fills Socrates' injunction to "know thyself," who is truthful—

if not necessarily in expression, at least in the grasp of their own dynamics. They might think of someone whose understanding and sympathy penetrate outward to the through-line of a situation, who is not triggered into capricious response by an isolated part of it. A deep person comprehends the totality that includes both self and world, what Coleridge called the "one life."

In what sense can we speak of the physical dimension of depth?

Humans are grown, not assembled. From a single cell we as embryos build up the amazing complexity of our bodies by dividing, again and again, and elaborating ever more intricate substructures. The same process may be viewed in our evolution as a species: elongation of the body, for instance, permitted turning, bending and coiling, which in turn evoked limbs for greater reach and mobility; arms grew themselves out into hands, and hands into fingers—formations which correspond to the discriminating intentions of a more complex nervous system. Both embryonic development and biological evolution are forms of self-expression that begin with a simple structure full of potentialities and then, by developing parts within parts within parts, manifest some of these potentialities in an amazing proliferation of details.

A finger is a refinement of the trunk, and we can grasp this inclusive relationship more clearly by comprehending the intervening layers of elaboration. A finger is part of a hand, which is part of a hand/forearm (a structural level for which we have no name), which is part of an upper limb, which is part of a shoulder girdle (including the upper limb as well as the shoulder itself), which is (to leap over a number of levels) part of a whole human person. If we view the relation of a finger to the person in this inclusive, layered way, we are thinking hierarchically—and we are concerned with depth.

Similarly, musicians may appreciate a symphonic movement by Mozart as an unfolding of a single pitch, the tonic. The motion of the music, its direction and meaning, can be understood as the relation of foreground (the actual sounding notes) to background (the tonic) through a series of levels. At the background level a whole composition elaborates the tonic into a progression from tonic to dominant and back to tonic. Each of the three steps of this progression is elaborated, and the elaborations are themselves elaborated, and so forth out to the furthest foreground level of the notes. The motion of the piece is not away from the tonic and then back to it, but is within the tonic. A musician who can "place" an individual note in its hierarchy of levels will hear its local melodic/harmonic function and expressive character embedded in the broader motion of the entire piece; the musical moment exists not as one in a string of isolated sound-events but as a particular instant, or instance, of the whole. To hear tonal music hierarchically, whether consciously or not, is to hear its depth, to listen through the single note to its roots and resonances within the whole piece.

We can illustrate the relevance of this hierarchical line of thought to everyday movement of life with the experience of Max, a pianist suffering from a chronic spasm in the fourth and fifth fingers of his right hand. The spasm itself afflicts only particular hand and forearm muscles, but their continuing overexertion is related to an imbalance of effort between hand, arm, and shoulder; the finger flexors are, in effect, presuming to do the job of larger and more powerful muscles further up the line. The pattern of effort in the shoulder musculature is a reflection, in turn, of the balance of forces around his spine, and this relates to the way he uses the bench and floor for support. Simply on the level of locomotor functioning, the nature of the structure generalizes the problem of the finger spasm. It cannot be solved, or even understood, as a local phenomenon.

The nervous system, like the musculoskeletal system, is organized hierarchically. The hand is innervated richly with connections to the higher centers of the brain, where more conscious, voluntary, thought-provoked action originates; in contrast, the muscles of the back, especially at deeper levels, are controlled more by the older, preconscious, reflexive centers.

And here we see that the generalizing of Max's pain problem does not stop with his neural and muscular systems, for the shape taken by his arms, shoulders, spine, and pelvis is expressive. Prior to his artistic work with the sounding instrument and the musical score, his body's movements manifest his particular pattern of hope, fear, anger, and love. Since childhood he has tended to be competitive in performance situations, with a strong desire to please others and elicit admiration from them. Even when rehearsing alone he feels pressure to avoid those wrong notes which lurk on the sidelines, ready to pounce into his performance if he lets down his guard. This pattern of psychological forces shapes his body: his taut back muscles arch him into a projected image of self-assurance. Simultaneously, they collaborate with arm and shoulder muscles in a watchful, on-guard pulling back of his elbows. This network of tensions precedes, underlies, and undercuts anything he may do to interpret the particular piece of music he is playing.

In his eagerness to make a good showing, Max has become almost exclusively absorbed in the action of his fingers against the piano keys; he more or less forgets that the rest of his body participates in playing and contributes to the support of his hands. He is preoccupied with the voluntary, manipulable end of his spectrum of neurological possibilities. You can hear this preoccupation in the music: his performance sounds calculated for effect and not shaped from a spontaneous response. To that extent his music loses its genuineness. Critics often comment that Max's playing, for all its technical brilliance, is unfeeling.

When you watch him, you can see this detachment. There is a lack of smooth coordination between his agile hands and his trunk, which appears to remain almost still, or lurches about in crude relationship to the music. The energy generated for striking the keys is isolated.

This is not to suggest that weaving and bobbing trunk movement will produce powerful or exquisite piano playing, nor to say that more movement is better than less. But an integration of arm and hand movement with the rest of the person respects the hierarchical nature of our structure and of the music itself, and will not only reduce stress but support a deeper and more authentic expressiveness.

To view Max's finger spasms hierarchically is to put them in context. On a physical level he can ease the strain by allowing his arm, shoulder, and trunk to participate appropriately and more fully in supporting the quicker and lighter action of the hand. On psychological and spiritual levels he can step back for a more comprehensive perspective on his motivations, letting the very problem guide him toward values that will be truer to himself.

Max's situation is typical of our hectic and driven culture. What we call tension is often unsupported peripheral muscular hyperactivity, characterized in Max's case by jerky, sudden, overresponsive action and in some cases by seeming slackness. Excessively willed, or willful, it emphasizes the most recent stages of our evolution at the expense of an older and deeper responsiveness. It defines the individual too sharply, often creating a feeling of isolation and of being overwhelmed by a chaos of stimuli. Sensing movement hierarchically is ecological, a deepening process which puts our activity into the context of its external and internal embedding.

Arms and shoulders are designed to hang from the spinal axis.

Chronic tension holds them up, against gravity.

Chapter 3

Lifted by Gravity

Mark the perfect man, and behold the upright:
For the end of that man is peace.
    Psalm 37:37 (*King James Version*)

Observe the innocent man, consider the upright:
for the man of peace there are descendants. . . .
    Psalm 37:37 (*The Jerusalem Bible*)

Experiencing Weight

Gymnasts, divers, acrobats, and ballet dancers throw their weight around, dramatizing, sometimes to the point of danger, a capacity to use the body's momentum. Perhaps we admire them in part because our ordinary movements share their play with weight—because sitting down in a chair also tosses the body through space.

This mundane movement, like their spectacular ones, is a chance to express vitality by letting body weight swing into an action. We can throw our weight when we reach out for things, when we walk, run, make music, or make love. Body weight is not just a burden to be dragged about as a punishment for gluttony and sloth but can be a profound and ever-deepening source of well-being, as Thomas's movement awareness class discovered one afternoon early in the semester.

It was near the end of the class, and they were reflecting on what they had been doing, a series of activities designed to bring them into an awareness of their weight. Helen was the first to speak. "It was interesting to lie on the floor and have Pam lift my arm so slowly, and then lower it back to the floor. Thomas, you told us not to help our partner lift the weight but to let the arm rest into their hands. I began to notice how I was anticipating the lift by tightening muscles deep in my arm. At first I couldn't stop. Finally I did let go and could feel the resting weight; at just that point Pam said 'Ah!' as if she had felt it too. Then, when we repeated the arm lifts standing up, I noticed how much effort I generally use to hold my shoulders and arms up. What a relief to let them hang down."

A quiet intimacy had developed in the group, and there was no hurry to break in on the reflective silence which followed Helen's comments.

Pam spoke. "When Helen began to lift my arm I was at first distracted, embarrassed to have her feel how heavy I am—I mean, how fat. But as Thomas coached us to experience weight, gradually I was able to stop worrying about Helen and to notice my own sensations. I was reminded of floating on my back in the lake by my family's summer cabin. As I released the weight, my arm seemed to lighten in Helen's hands. A similar thing happened when she lifted each leg: as I let go of tension, my arms and legs felt more a part of me, not just tacked on. At the end, when you asked us to walk around the room and notice whatever we felt, it seemed as though my legs were more underneath my body when I took each step. They felt stronger and not so clumsy as I moved. I felt less chubby."

Helen broke in. "It's peculiar, but what you registered as your arm being lighter seemed more like weight to me. Your arm let itself fall into my hands."

"You run into paradoxes in this work," said Thomas. "Words are not adequate to the experience. Certainly we are dealing with weight here—I'm sure you could measure it with scales. Yet the very same quality also might be described as lightness: you let go of something, and it rests down so that its weight is more palpable, but at the same time there isn't the effort of holding it up."

Josh spoke. "I was noticing something similar when we were lying down and giving attention to our breathing. Thomas asked us to experience the weight of the breastbone being lifted by inhalation and then resting downward on exhalation as if it were a chip of wood on the ocean. I discovered that I would cut off the end of each exhalation before it came to a natural finish, and then hurry into the next breath, anticipating it and not allowing the weight of the chip to settle fully at the the end of the breath. The more I allowed the breaths to have their full moment—or rather, the more I gave my attention to the very end of each exhalation, not trying to make it happen but just perceiving it—the more apparent was the sensation of weight. But when I stood up afterwards, I felt as if a weight had been taken off my chest." Josh paused. "Noticing my own weight gave me a sense of being closer to myself, yet also less self-conscious."

Thomas recalled his earliest observations of these students, three weeks before. Pam's body, somewhat overweight, drooped as she stood and sat. Long cardigans and loosely fitted skirts suggested she was hiding what she considered an excess of flesh. Yet the initial impression of ponderousness resulted more from slack organization than from excess pounds. Her spritely good humor, which expressed a lighter and more orderly side of herself, filtered into view only after one had been with her for a time.

Helen, Pam's partner this afternoon, was average in build, with a gaze and a style of comment in class that bespoke personal intensity, but she gave the initial impression of being frail and insubstantial—a pushover. She held her shoulders drawn forward and up and pulled herself in around her chest; there was a pronounced furrow between her eyebrows.

If Pam's weight was slumped and Helen's insubstantial, Josh's was hardened and impenetrable. He looked as though he might have attended military school and retained the imprint of postures learned there: shoulders back, arms and legs rigid, chin elevated. But his keen and scientific remarks in class showed a free-wheeling imagination that flickered through the physical impactedness.

A lack of feeling for their own weight, expressed in such different outward forms, linked the three. It stood in the way of their assuming a fuller, freer, and more natural stature. And it masked strengths of spirit and self-expression that might shine forth more clearly as they allowed their weight to function creatively.

In the weeks following these simple experiences, Thomas continued working with his class on the perception of weight, and he saw changes in each of them. Pam's walk lessened its side-to-side sway. As she herself had noticed, her legs swung more directly under her torso. Her head and chest rode higher and the bulge of her abdomen was slimmer, as if her weight had been gathered closer to her central axis where it was better supported. Helen gained in solidity; with lowered and more pliable shoulders, her weight seemed more in touch with the floor. Her frown softened. Josh eased; his arms hung at his sides, swinging as he walked, and his chest, which had been puffed-out and held high, was more mobile as he breathed. A quality of tenderness surfaced. Thomas was once again amazed that something as simple as awareness of weight could produce such a breadth and depth of consequences.

The attention of these students was being focused on a perception, not on an idea, and Helen, Pam, and Josh all reported some difficulty with this. Many of us would share the same difficulty. We do not usually concentrate on simple kinesthetic experience, and unless the body and its movements give us pain or intense pleasure, sensation is buried in a welter of preoccupations.

To search for and sustain an interest in one's own weight—the weight of an arm, shoulder, or leg—may at first stir up a clutter of unpleasant associations. It may, as it did for Pam, bring up the issue of fat. Or there may be a more generalized connection of weight with effort and strain—carrying the groceries in from the car, or hurrying with suitcases down long airport corridors. Furthermore, the very tensions which hold up weight also conceal themselves; muscular tension is white noise in the nervous system, and we become habituated to it.

Before his experiences with weight, if Josh had been asked to name the opposite of "tension," his answer would have been "relaxation," a term which to him implied being laid back. But he came to see that "weight" would be another appropriate answer, and that released weight contributes to the vigor and commitment of action as well as to fullness of rest.

Weight as the Opposite of Tension

If you deliberately tighten your arms and shoulders, hold the tension for a few seconds, then slowly release, you will feel your arms drawn downward by gravity. The shoulders will follow, eased away from neck and head by their own weight and by the weight of your arms. At some point the muscles will have returned to the tonus they had before you tightened them. If you then continue giving attention to the experience of weight, you will find that the muscles can continue releasing, not because you are actively doing something to or with them but purely in response to your awareness of weight. You are using your perception of weight to reduce tension below your habitual operating level. By repeating the experience you can progressively lower that habitual level. This may seem too obvious and inexpensive a procedure to be of much value, but when coupled with awareness of balance, it can be the basis for a sustained unknitting of tension habits.

The perception of one's own weight is a healing process; it directs us toward wholeness and integration. Before her experience in the movement awareness class, Pam would have said just the opposite because she was not perceiving her weight but thinking it—holding the image of herself as fat and unattractive and reacting to that image. Thomas encouraged her to break away from fascination with the image, to redirect attention to sensation in order to gain a different perspective.

Being aware of weight is not *doing* anything, not imaging or even actively relaxing, but simply directing attention to a sensation which is always accessible. The only active control exerted is in the focus of attention. One learns to slip in and out of the perception of weight, to melt through the identification with an all-too-familiar style of contraction, and to let the sensation of suspended, swinging weight be operative as the background of all activity.

Awareness of weight can be a form of meditation, practiced not only when sitting still but while going about daily pursuits. If Josh were to reach out to touch something—say, to answer the telephone—and if as he moved he continued to experience the weight of his arm, that awareness would counteract his habitual tendency to overcontract the muscles of his arm and shoulder. If while talking to her chemistry teacher Helen were to notice that her own face was rigidly set in an uneasy grin, simple awareness of the weight of her jaw and of the flesh of her cheeks could ease her facial muscles into a more authentic expression. If while walking Pam were to feel the weight of her swinging leg draw space into the hip joint, she would be practicing peace of mind as well as a more efficient style of motion.

The Body as a Pendent Structure

Though excess tension is generally recognized as a destructive habit, there is at the same time a prejudice, often unconscious, that good posture is an act of will requiring a constant effort of muscular tension, and that we will necessarily sag into bad posture as soon as attention is turned elsewhere. The fact is that when a body is in balance, release of weight leads to greater buoyancy and facilitates an upright carriage. By nature the body is a pendent structure. It hangs on its supportive framework, and the less one interferes by chronic tension, the more efficiently the supportive framework operates and the more peaceful a home it provides.

Take the rib cage as an example: a pair of ribs articulates with each of the spinal vertebrae of the upper back and is suspended by bands of ligament, muscle, and tendon that angle upward from each rib to the vertebrae above (p. 35, A). These braces of rib arc around to the front of the chest where pliable cartilage links them together into the vertical shaft of the breastbone (p. 35, B and D). Each pair of ribs is like a bucket handle rotating around points of articulation on each side of the spine (p. 35, C). Inhalation fills the lungs not only by pulling down on the diaphragm but by lifting the bucket handles and widening this loose network of ribs. Exhalation is a release of muscular action which allows gravity to draw the bucket handles down again on their spinal pivots.

Chronic tension may prevent gravity from returning the structure, during exhalation, to its pendency; rather than fully releasing their lift of the rib cage, muscles continue partially holding it up. Inhalation never entirely passes into exhalation. The depth of breathing—its success in replacing one lungful of air with another—is a measure not simply of the peak of inhalation but of the valley of completed exhalation and of the distance between the two. To release the weight of the rib cage during exhalation, to allow it to settle fully, is to establish the emptiness from which the next breath can most generously arise.

Like the rib cage, the shoulder girdle is a pendent structure, partly slung from the spine and the back of the head,

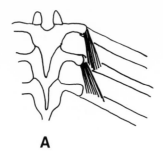

A

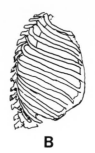

B

C

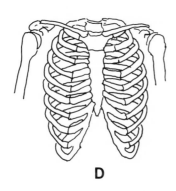

D

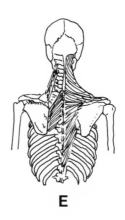

E

partly perched on the hanging thorax (p. 35, E). The collarbones—two struts anchored at their medial ends to the top of the breastbone—are suspended from the back of the neck and skull, particularly by the trapezius muscle, which also suspends the shoulder blades.

From the lateral edges of the shoulder blades (the shoulder sockets) hang the arms themselves. The weight of the arms draws collarbones and shoulder blades down, away from head and neck. Gravity returns the trapezius and related muscles to their resting state after they have completed an action. In other words, the weight of the arms restores full length to the muscles, and they are prepared to act again with maximum effect. If you shrug your shoulders in an "I don't know" gesture, arm weight completes the gesture. Chronic tension, *carrying* the weight rather than letting it hang, is an effort that produces no movement. In fact, it interferes with movement by preempting the muscles. "I don't know" goes on and on, forgotten but still expressed, and piles itself on top of succeeding actions.

The thorax and shoulder girdle are two parts of the body that most obviously show its pendent nature. Another is the leg as it swings forward; the leg hangs from the hip, and awareness of its weight can enhance the action of the swing in walking or running.

Tensegrity and Weight

Weight not only hangs on the rack of the skeleton but is itself part of the support system. To understand how weight participates in support, it is instructive to look at the tensegrity structure, an architectural creation of Buckminster Fuller. Its coherence is determined by the inward pull of tensional members (a network of wires, cables, strings, or rubber

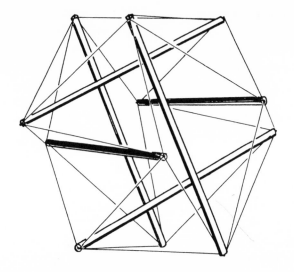

bands under tension) resisted by compressional members (sticks, steel girders) which enforce space by thrusting outward.

To think clearly about the human body as a tensegrity structure we need to distinguish between muscle tissue and connective tissue. Whereas muscle tissue has the power to change its length and therefore to exert a pull, connective tissue—ligament, tendon, fascia—is passive. Ligaments bind joints in order to allow and at the same time limit movement. Fascia and tendons mediate between the contracting capacity of muscle tissue and the rigidity of bone: they are the ropes on which muscle pulls in order to apply its force to bone. Fascia both penetrates and envelops muscle tissue, honeycombing its way around tiny muscle cells, groups of cells, muscles, and muscle groups; it condenses into sheets (aponeuroses) and cords (tendons), distributing or gathering the energy of muscle action.

If we leave out of the picture for a moment the muscle tissue, with its capacity to change length, the bone-and-connective-tissue system has the look of a tensegrity structure, with bones corresponding to the sticks (compression members) and connective tissue to the wires (tension members). The skeleton is not, in this picture, a stack of solid blocks transmitting accumulated weight down through the column, but a series of spacers floating in the tensional network and allowing it to distribute its forces. Bones never quite meet; joints are not frictional contacts, but articulations. Stephen M. Levine, an orthopedic physician who has investigated the relevance of the tensegrity model to the human body, wrote that

> although some of the rigid components of a tensegrity system may "kiss," it does not mean that they are in compressive opposition to one another. Axial loads were applied to joints in live subjects under anesthesia during surgical intervention for a variety of conditions. Joint studies included the knee, ankle, elbow and metatarsal-phalangeal joints. In our studies at no time could the articular surfaces of these joints be forced into contact with one another as long as the ligaments remained intact. (Levine 1982, 33; see also Kirkby 1975)

Still speaking of this "pre-movement" picture, without muscle action, the integrity of the body's structure is tensional: the connective tissue exerts an inward pull that not only keeps the parts together but (because of the resistance of the bones to compression) lifts the whole structure upward against gravity. When you assemble a tensegrity model like the icosahedron pictured above, it remains a loose tangle of sticks and wires lying on the table until the last two or three connections of wires and sticks are made; then the network of opposed tensional and compressional forces lifts it up and creates space within it.

Body weight, by pulling downward, activates the integrative network. If you press any one point on a tensegrity model the whole structure "talks back": every wire meets the pressure somewhat the way a balloon—the whole balloon, not just the point touched—presses back if a finger is pushed into it. Weight pulling down on the body is like a pressing or pulling force applied all over the structure, creating a tensional response which is in part upward against gravity. The tension is a passive response of the connective tissue network, not the biological action of muscle contraction. Since the response is from the whole system, weight is integrative.

The human body more closely resembles a tensegrity *mast* than a single more or less spherical structure. A tensegrity mast is a vertical interweaving of individual tensegrity cells. The spine, with its tapestry of soft tissues built up around the out-thrusting bony processes of each vertebra, bears a striking resemblance.

Muscle tissue, with its capacity to create movement, fits into this light gridwork. By pulling selectively on the tensional net of connective tissue, muscles change the spatial relationship of parts. They also contribute to the integrity of the system by creating tonus, a constant activity that pulls the structure together. But therein lie the seeds of a problem: when muscles are overactive in their toning function they disrupt and overpower the lifting action of weight. Josh, when he focused attention on the settling of his sternum as he exhaled, let go of an increment of muscular tension so that his tensegrity system was allowed to operate more freely. He felt his chest lighten. Pam, releasing the tension in her limbs, experienced the tensegrity network connecting them to the rest of her.

Weight acts on connective tissue in a way different from, and in some respects contrary to, muscular action. Where

39

weight tends to lengthen structures and open joints, muscular action shortens and closes them. As we have seen, the weight of the arms pulls the shoulders down; that is, it lengthens the distance between the shoulders and the neck and opens the shoulder joints themselves. Muscular contraction acting in the same structures pulls the shoulders up toward the head and draws the upper arms into the shoulder sockets.

Tensegrity structures reverberate: if you drop one on the floor it will bounce. The quality of the bounce depends on the degree of tension in the wires: a loose weave produces a marshmallowy, sagging bounce which absorbs the impact, while a more tightly woven model springs higher and will bounce again and again. Tightening the wires even more will make a rigid and unyielding structure. In bodies, a movement anywhere will send out a wave of response through the structure: the whole body participates, and the better organized it is around the skeletal core, the more clearly it reverberates. A person whose musculature is either slack or bound by excessive tension cannot act either as delicately or as powerfully as one that reverberates more freely.

The tensegrity model of the human body is not, as presented here, a rigorous scientific hypothesis. But it can operate as an elegant and evocative metaphor, organizing the understanding of experiences that are poorly accounted for by the assumption that bodies operate as compression structures. Its chief value is as a *via negativa*, which breaks up habitual assumptions that hold us entranced and unable to perceive ourselves directly. It allows us to explore the possibility that experiencing body weight and allowing it free play in movement respects our design and therefore expresses us with less wear and tear and with more efficiency and pleasure.

An understanding of tensegrity changes the meaning of the statement that "the body is a pendent structure." We are not flesh hanging on a rack of bone, but an interplay of forces where the soft tissue itself contributes to support. Gravity can actually lift the body, lengthening it skyward and at the same time easing its actions. Awareness of balanced weight is a direct, utterly simple means for giving ourselves back to gravity.

Chapter 4

Balance

Yes; but you must wager. It is not optional. You are
embarked. Which will you choose then? Let us see.
Blaise Pascal, *Pensées* (1670) 1931, 66

Balance around the Vertical Axis

Immersed as we are in the earth's gravitational field, we cannot help but respond to it. Will we choose to be lifted by its
vertical thrust through our bodies? Or will we let it drag on
us? Or will we withhold ourselves rigidly from its benefits?
Full stature, with its delicacy and power of action, depends
on whether we center our physical structure close to the vertical axis by aligning head, chest, abdomen, pelvis, legs, and
feet along the force vector of gravity that plunges down
through us.

By far the most common response of people who come

into better balance is "I feel lighter." This is true even when one of the pathways to balance has been the experience of resting body weight into its frame of support. We can see the same lightness-in-weight in an old-fashioned pair of scales, where pans hang down from a horizontal beam that pivots across a fulcrum.

When the weights and the distance from the fulcrum are equal, the weights seem to float. If you tap one of the pans, the horizontal beam and both pans will move and then oscillate back to stillness. But if you increase the weight in one of the pans, or suspend it closer to the fulcrum, that pan will fall until it rests against something solid. The floating dynamic of counterbalance is lost. A weighing scale, were it sentient, might say that it felt lighter when its weights were in balance.

Scales are not ordinarily tensegrity structures, but they could be. If the center post were a mast made up of interconnected tensegrity modules stacked vertically, as we have surmised the human spine to be, not only would the pan on the left counterbalance that on the right but their equilibrium would balance the forces throughout the central mast itself. Applying the image to the human body, the counterbalancing of parts—left and right, front and back—allows the tensional network itself, the whole muscular system, to function with less effort.

Being a highly flexible structure, upended in gravity with a narrow unstable base, the human body is constantly adjust-

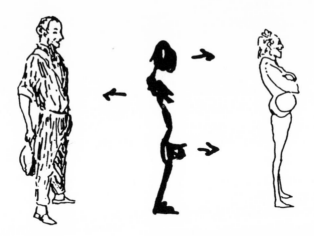

ing its parts to take advantage of counterbalancing. If the pelvis shifts to the right, the shoulder girdle or some other part will shift to the left. We make these reverberative adjustments, involving every part of the body, whenever we move, and as momentary accommodations they are the means by which we maintain the most favorable possible relationship to gravity. But when segments of the body are more or less permanently displaced from their efficient alignment—when a habitually forward-thrusting head, for example, calls for adjustments of the shoulder girdle, the rib cage, the pelvis and all the rest of the body—gravity becomes a dragging or wearing force because we have lost our favorable alignment along the vertical axis.

Repeated actions, particularly when they involve carrying or lifting added weight, may turn into postural distortions. A child who carries a load of books around school every day, snugging them up against her chest and wrapping herself around them, may "forget" to regain her simple relationship to the vertical when she puts the books down. The carrying action, once a momentary arrangement for a specific purpose, becomes ensnared in the flesh as postural, part of her character stance.

We have seen how values, attitudes, and emotional habits can shape our weight-bearing into sustained distortions. Traumatic accidents, serious illnesses, and developmental anomalies—what Ida Rolf called randomizing influences—also establish patterns of accommodation that spread throughout the body and implant themselves there. Someone who has had a right hip replaced will probably shift more weight to the left leg, requiring compensatory adjustments throughout the entire musculoskeletal network.

If the center of gravity of the head is carried several inches in front of the body's axis, as is frequently the case, all head movements are correspondingly more ponderous. Since the body automatically—reflexively—counterbalances weight, the forward carriage of the head is usually reflected in a pulling backward of the rib cage, which then also requires a higher energy output for movement. And so forth on down through the body's whole system of weight compensations: a retracted rib cage is usually compensated by a forward carriage not only of the head but of the abdomen and pelvis.

Another way of accounting for the destructive effects of

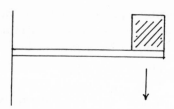

gravity on imbalanced bodies is to consider the cantilever. If you build a house on the edge of a cliff and part of the structure hangs out beyond the edge supported by horizontal beams, those beams are cantilevers. Cantilevers must be rigid. When the head rides out in front of its spinal support, the neck must act in part as a cantilever, and to that extent it stiffens—that is, its joints become immobile and the system of muscle, bone, nerve, and connective tissue designed for exquisite shades of movement is co-opted for the cruder task of holding weight. Any other part of the body that has shifted away from the vertical axis will require stiffening for support.

You can feel the contrast between crude and nuanced head movement in a simple experiment. Imagine a gnat flying around in front of your face. Follow its quick darting with your chin jutted forward, and notice the quality of your head and neck movements. Now perch your head directly above your trunk. Watch the same gnat, and notice the increased delicacy and variety in the movements.

Imbalance almost always shortens a body; improving the vertical alignment lengthens it. The three primary curves of the spine (concave toward the rear in the lower back and in the neck, and convex toward the rear in the thorax) are softened (that is, flattened) as the pelvis, chest, and head align themselves vertically over the arches of the feet.

The centers of gravity of the parts and of the body as a whole ride higher when the spine is less deeply curved. Weight is poised, ready to fall into activity; potential energy is stored in this lifted weight. The physical attitude is an alert readiness for contingencies, and when the person moves into action there is space for an adaptive, reverberative flow of adjustment from one joint to another, particularly along the spine.

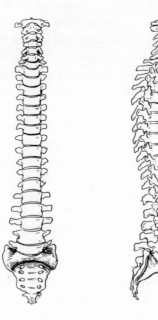

In addition to feeling lighter, a common response when a person discovers a more balanced stature is "I feel open." The delight is often flecked with a certain apprehension, for on the nether side of our wish to be open and available to others is a caution about being too exposed.

Thomas often began his movement classes by coaching his students to rock slowly between balance and imbalance and finally to settle into a comfortable vertical alignment. At the end of this quieting adventure with internal sensations he was always touched by the shine of good-willed humanness and emergent energy in the group standing together at full stature. Frequently this unaccustomed openness created a shyness among them. When the class went on to the next exploration some would draw back into their familiar postural shell, and much of his work with them—their work with themselves—was to bring awareness to this habit of withdrawal so that they could begin to unravel it.

The openness of the body, a spaciousness particularly of the organ chamber which lies in front of the spine, depends upon our centering body weight so that the vertical axis runs more or less through the spine, and weight bearing and movement are therefore managed by the locomotor system. Slouching, both standing and sitting, brings the weight of the head to bear down through the lungs, heart, and digestive system. Organs are required to resist this constant downward force, a function for which they are not designed and which interferes with their normal activities. An exaggerated arching backward of the spine, on the other hand, though it may open the front of the trunk, rigidifies the torso and limits movement.

Balance involves a slight forward tilt of the body so that weight is centered in the arches of the feet, a little in front of the ankles. Since the head is somewhat heavier in front of its fulcrum than behind, muscular tone is required in the back of the neck simply to keep the head from falling forward. The body's slight forward tilt evokes this toning all the way down the back: the weight of the head and of the front of the trunk exerts a gentle forward pull which lengthens the spine, drawing space particularly into the neck and the lower back rather than compressing stolidly downward. The attitude is alert, mobilized, receptive, and peaceful.

 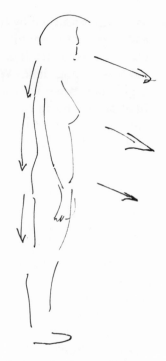

Toning the body by finding its designed relationship to the vertical orientation of gravity is like tuning a violin; it brings the parts into a harmonious relationship with one another. What is established by tuning is not simply an arbitrary set of preconceived relationships but a world of creative possibilities, the world of tonality. The pitches have rightness (in an older parlance, "righteousness"), an aliveness to one another, and a hierarchical context that gives them depth, meaning, and feeling. Balancing oneself in gravity is similarly creative—not simply a more efficient and healthful way to behave but a homecoming to the harmonious interrelatedness that is our birthright. It readies us to play the creative options provided by life.

Balance is a center around which movement orients itself, not a static position. Even the relative stillness of standing and sitting is marked by movement: the subtle play of our righting reflexes gently sways us back to center, from which we constantly swing away again in tiny oscillations. This dance of the structure is particularly comforting when balance has poised the body's weight in its inherent lightness. A deliberate gentle swaying, perhaps to music, can help one explore the flexible nature of balance. Just to take a moment to come into sitting balance, then to sway around and through centered alignment, can be a refreshment and a reminder of supportive resources.

The whole person participates in balance: everything adjusts to everything else so that no segment can be understood apart from this interactive whole. Nevertheless, it will be useful at this point to survey how particular parts of the body express balance and imbalance, keeping in mind that we are talking about them as local, but not isolated, phenomena.

Pelvis and Low Back

As we have seen, the most common pattern of imbalance positions the pelvis in front of its optimal relationship to both the legs and the chest.

The rib cage usually responds by leaning backward and down, where it resists forward movement and contributes a feeling of heaviness and immobility to the body. Shifting the pelvis backward into the line of the body's central axis and more securely under the weight of the upper body allows a sturdier and smoother transmission of support from the feet and legs to the spine, rib cage, and head.

The forward carriage of the pelvis seems to be a cultural inheritance, a form of original sin that pervades our so-called higher civilization. With it goes a predisposition toward low back and sacroiliac pain. The deepening of the lumbar curve (lordosis, or swayback), by dropping upper body weight behind where it can be efficiently supported, squeezes the posterior part of the spinal disks. Movement under such compression increases wear and tear on disks, and their degeneration then threatens the free space needed for the spinal cord and for the nerves which thread their way between the vertebrae as they branch out from the spinal cord.

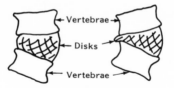

An archer's bow, where a string is attached to the ends of a flexible stick and tightened to bend the stick into an arc, illustrates what happens in a human body: the bones of the thighs, pelvis, and lower spine correspond to the stick and the posterior muscles to the string. The realignment of the skeleton is in large part a matter of relaxing this taut string.

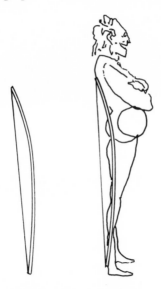

The carriage of the pelvis in front of its optimal relationship to the legs and chest is associated with chronic tension in the muscles of the buttocks and this in turn with organic complications here in the psychologically freighted location of elimination and reproduction. Some of the complexes identified long ago by Freud—anal retention and various forms of sexual dysfunction—are related to chronic holding of pelvic muscles.

The forward displacement of the pelvis in standing is often associated with its simultaneous tilting, so that the pelvic bowl is lower in front than in back. Since the sacrum—the lower portion of the spine—is firmly embedded in the pelvis, the pelvic tilt is a sacral tilt as well, and deepens swayback. In sitting, the slumped tilt of the pelvis is usually in the opposite direction, with the sacrum leaning backward at the top; the body counterbalances by throwing upper body weight forward so that the spine makes a C-curve facing forward.

Sacrum

Habitual sustained tilting of the pelvis, whether forward or backward, sitting or standing or moving, deprives the upper body of a secure foundation.

Occasionally the pelvis positions itself behind its most supportive relationship to the rib cage, so that the lumbar curve is too flat for flexible movement and for an efficient line of support.

Abdomen

In our four-footed cousins the organs hang down from the spine; the locomotor system operates around them, leav-

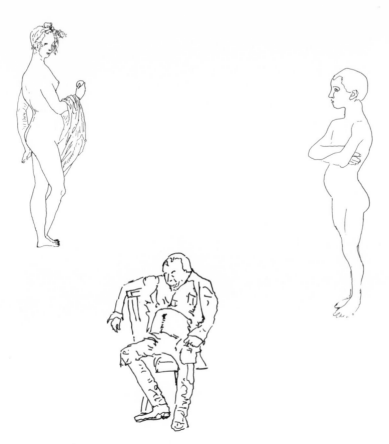

ing them free for their own functions. Our upended style of mobility is more complex, and organs can, with a shift of balance, easily be asked to assume the inappropriate role of carrying weight. A slouched posture, as we have seen, drops upper body weight through the chest and abdomen.

The abdominal wall is designed to span the distance between rib cage and pelvis with a protective enclosure that passes the responsibility for support and movement around the circumference of the organ chamber. Swayback pushes organs forward against the abdominal wall, which bulges out and at the same time tightens to hold its contents. The resultant shape leads to a tragicomic vicious circle in our figure-conscious world. The bulging is often interpreted as limpness, and the conclusion frequently follows that "building" these muscles—that is, tightening them up—will pull the abdomen into place. Hence, situps, leg lifts, and "suck in your gut." But when the abdominal muscles are chronically shortened by these disciplined efforts, the rib cage and the pelvis are pulled closer together and then held that way; the lower spine must also shorten, which it can do only by deepening its swayback curve, pushing the organs with still more force against the abdominal wall. The difficulty in this self-defeating circle lies not in the practice of toning the muscles, which may need it, but in approaching the problem outside its postural context and not recognizing that balance is an essential ingredient for dealing with the errant bulge. The lower spine needs to lengthen by shifting backward in order that the front may flatten.

Many organic maladies can improve in response to a systematic rebalancing of structure: ulcers, chronic constipation, and premenstrual syndrome to mention only a few. Premenstrual syndrome, for example, is evidently related to the cyclical alteration of hormone balance and perhaps to psychological upbringing. Whatever the particular factors may be, one symptom is a recurrent increase of general muscular tension which is also reflected as a change in posture. The body is pulled into a more stressful relationship to gravity, most likely an increase in swayback. Imbalance then steps up the tension by requiring more effort for support and movement, which increases the pain, which produces more tension, and so forth, into the swirl of that syndrome. If, prior to the ups and downs of cyclical change, the overall level of abdominal and back tension is lowered by an improvement of balance, the cyclical change, though it still involves an increase in tension, may not be sufficient to drive the person into pain. Improved balance may also influence premenstrual syndrome by way of its emotional dimension: an easier and more flexible balance is a different psychological stance, which at the same time is reflected in the hormonal balance.

Legs and Feet

When the upper body is balanced, walking is a pleasure. Rhythmic leg and arm swings propel us through space to an inner beat which is expressed by weight meeting the earth: rolling through the heel, being absorbed and distributed across the arch and being pushed off from the toes. The arch of the foot is a custom-designed shock absorber, a collection of small bones knitted together with elastic bands of muscle and connective tissue and arranged in a canopy shape. It flattens slightly under the body's weight and then arches slightly to help push off that weight from the toes. This innately supple foot feels out and adapts itself to the more unyielding surfaces of the earth.

The shortening of the back has a variety of consequences for the legs and feet. We have seen, with the image of the archer's bow, how contraction of the posterior musculature generally extends down the legs and participates in pulling upper body weight behind its optimal line of balance.

Imagine these figures walking. The pronounced counter-balancing of forward pelvis with backward-leaning rib cage gives the impression that the walk is being contradicted by the upper body lagging behind. The weight thuds into the heels and becomes stuck there, not easily able to spill forward across the foot. Since the heel is solid bone, it passes the shock up the shafts of the leg bones to the spine which, if its bowing is exaggerated, is already under strain and not favorably disposed for distributing the impact.

Michael, a timpanist, walked heavily on his heels. He was a rather contentious fellow who, to his own distress, sometimes made enemies among the other orchestra members by his unpredictable spells of irritation. Alert to sound, Michael had a good ear for the subtle timbral distinctions possible on the timpani and other percussion instruments. Oddly enough, he had been oblivious to the percussive sounds of his own walking and jogging. One day in rehearsal he became aware of his thudding heels as he walked, pelvis thrust forward, across the stage of the concert hall; he contrasted it with the sound made when he shifted his pelvis backward and his rib cage forward and allowed his lower back to lengthen. He was surprised at the aesthetic difference. The dry dull thumps of imbalance reminded him of playing on the wrong part of the drumhead; walking in balance, his feet drew a lighter and livelier resonance out of the floor, just as his mallets did when they struck the best spot on the drumhead. The musical quality of his walking became a cue for balancing his walk.

Having observed his walking, he quickly awakened to the jarring impact of his feet slapping the ground when he jogged. He discovered how shifting his weight forward—by releasing tension between the shoulder blades and allowing his back to soften and lengthen—changed his contact with the ground into gentler and more articulate foot-strokes.

Sound also became a cue for Michael to monitor the episodes of irritation that got him into trouble with his colleagues. One day in a movement workshop Thomas asked him to "walk angrily." Without thinking, Michael assumed an exaggerated version of his familiar pattern of imbalance, and there came the heel thuds, duller than ever. When he was asked to "walk happily" he shifted toward balance and resonance was restored. He later reported being able to anticipate his spells of irritation, to hear them coming and steer himself clear.

What often passes for standing is a lean of the body against itself. In one characteristic version, feet are spread

and legs locked into place at the knee and hip joints, the arms folded on the belly's ledge, the curves of the spine deepened so that the vertebrae are compressed: the person leans on the abdomen, on the ligaments across the front of the hip, and on the tendons and ligaments across the back of the knee. In another kind of lean, one side of the body anchors itself down through leg and foot while the other side drapes against it, leg and foot propped a bit in front and splayed outward. These leans, in which the effort of standing is unevenly concentrated, may become uncomfortable quickly; even in a brief period an uneasy restlessness will shift us from leg to leg in the array of variations an individual has developed.

In balanced standing, mobility is potent: joints throughout the body are stable but not braced. The upper body poises upon a narrow base. Feet—toes pointing straight ahead—are

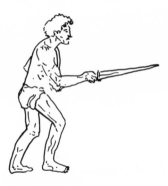

close together, roughly 2 or 3 inches apart (or a little further depending on the height and girth of the person) so that body weight, evenly distributed between right and left feet, is concentrated over the arches, on the medial part of each arch— between the heel and the big toe. A spread-out stance, feet wide apart, robs the standing body of appropriate support from the arches and legs and is generally associated with swayback, rotated (turned-out) legs, and locked knees. In simple relaxed standing, the relative instability and high center of gravity of a narrow base gives free play to the slight motions needed for breathing, speaking, and turning the head to hear and see; it also allows us to embark easily into walking or reaching. A wider stance with some hip and knee flexion, mobilizing the power of the large muscles, is appropriate when vigorous action—to throw a ball or pick up a heavy bag—is likely to call the body off its vertical axis.

Contraction of the back involves not only the deeper vertical muscles of the spine itself but the large surface muscles of the buttocks and back—gluteus maximus and lattissimus dorsi, which span diagonally into the arms and legs. When these large diagonal muscles are under chronic tension they not only contribute to the shortening of the back but also narrow it and, by pulling on their limb attachments, twist arms and legs into rotation. The result is not always a simple one of turning the thigh or the upper arm outward, because compensatory counterbalancing forces are also set up which may ultimately overpower the outward rotation—as, for example, when the thighs rotate inward into a knock-knee pattern.

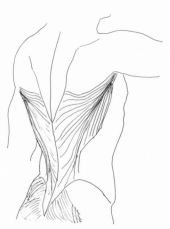

When rotational forces point the feet outward, walking and running pass body weight in a diagonal path from the outside of the heel to the inside of the big toe rather than directly down the axis of the foot. The toes are forced to propel body weight not by a simple push with their undersides, which have evolved for the purpose, but partly with their medial edges, which have not. The big toe, pushed sideways toward the other toes, may develop bunions; the medial arch of the foot, designed for meeting longitudinal stresses, is forced to bear the weight in this diagonal rolling pattern (outside of heel to inside of big toe), and often falls inward and flattens. Not just the foot but the entire body loses resiliency and power because it fails to meet the earth effectively.

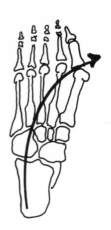 

When, on the other hand, the feet and knees both point straight forward into the direction of travel, and body weight is delivered in a line from the center of the heel to the big toe, the medial arch functions according to its design. Relearning the balanced use of the foot can build arches even in people who have been flat-footed since childhood.

Knees suffer from imbalance in a number of ways. They generally lock when the weight of the upper body is concentrated behind rather than over them: the lower legs are pulled behind the thighs by muscles that are holding the off-balance weight above them. The joint-faces and cartilages of the knees are put under inappropriate stress.

Locked (hyperextended) knees, like flat feet, are a sign of imbalance. It is possible to teach oneself to stand with flexed knees, but if the weight of the upper body is appropriately aligned, the knees will poise themselves, neither flexed nor hyperextended, in readiness to use the power of either flexion or extension in movement.

Knees are hinged front to back, and they are gradually injured by the rotational forces associated with a shortened lower spine. Knock-knees and bowlegs deprive a person of secure support, as anyone knows who has seen or felt these twists straighten: not only do the legs and feet come to operate more efficiently, but the upper body gains a lifted vitality that bears witness to a more supportive contact with the earth.

Rib Cage

The thorax is a hanging structure suspended from the back and floating protectively around its delicate and vulnerable cargo of internal organs. It functions as part of the shoulder girdle, which rests on the sternum at the medial ends of the collarbones. The force of arm and hand actions is then transmitted down the sternum and around the rib shafts to the spine. In addition to this floating line of skeletal support, the thorax furnishes attachments for many of the muscles which cross from the arm to the trunk, and it thereby keeps the locomotor activity of the arms and hands from interfering with the functioning of the lungs and heart. The design of the system calls for the organ chamber—lungs, heart, liver, digestive system, reproductive organs—to be free of weight-bearing responsibility. The organs hang on the front of the spine, and though our motor activities communicate with them, gently kneading, wringing, and pumping them, the work of locomotion is appropriately centered behind them in the spine. The rib cage also participates, somewhat like a bellows, in the movements of breathing.

A simple typology will be useful at this point, though in real life its distinctions are interwoven with one another in such intricate ways that it would be a mistake to take it too literally. Given an imbalance where the rib cage rides behind its optimal pelvic support, the chest can either sag or be puffed out by excessive muscular contraction. The sagging rib cage, which brings the person into a self-protective, self-involved attitude, appears to be anxiously withdrawing, the thrust-out rib cage to be anxiously aggressive.

The two types will not be seen in a pure state: most of us have built up layers that contrast with, or even contradict, one another, as Wilhelm Reich pointed out and as psychotherapists experience when they work through these layers with their clients—shyness giving way perhaps to anger, then sadness, then anxiety, then anger again, uncovering a history of successive styles like an archaeologist in a rich dig. We respond not only to our environment but to our own responses, changing course on the basis of our experience. If we fail to achieve a full integration of a particular stage of behavior—that is, if we in part repress it—we will leave a residue of expressive (meaningful or characterological) chronic tension that participates in the new response style. A woman who overcomes her timidity by developing a loud voice and tough stance may carry her old feeling of insecurity in the tension pattern of her shoulders, chest, and neck, and of course this pattern informs, or betrays, the very aggressiveness of her voice and stance.

And so a person is not unlikely to be afflicted with chronic forms of both aggression and withdrawal: we can droop our shoulders forward and at the same time pin them back. We can lash out in anger and at the same time withdraw in fear. Indeed, it is the nature of such patterns of tension to embody self-contradiction—to waste energy pulling one part against another in order to negate or water down the resulting expression, like magnets locking one another into immobility by the interaction of their force fields. The spatial relationships between parts—between, say, a forward-thrusting head, a drawn-back chest, and a hanging-out belly and pelvis—map the energies trapped in the system and reveal the connection of this internal energy system to the oceanic environment of gravity.

The postural shaping of the rib cage results in characteristic patterns of restricted breathing. The depressed rib cage applies an external force: the weight of the head bears down on the chest. Muscles that expand the thorax for inhalation are preoccupied by the need to resist this downthrust of misplaced weight. On the other hand a stiff, overexpanded rib cage, by requiring back and chest muscles to hold up the weight of the thorax itself, is also obstructed in its breathing capacity.

Head

The head, a heavy object perched on top of an unstable, flexible, softly S-curved vertical shaft, presents an ongoing challenge. Forward carriage of the head, which is common among us, can be associated with many different problems,

including headaches, neck pain, disturbed vision, and jaw tension. Sometimes the chin juts out so that the base of the skull is compressed into the back of the neck. Sometimes the plane of the face tilts down so that the throat is squeezed. A downward tilt aims the eyes at a closer point and narrows the field, a style of visual perception associated with a narrowing

of consciousness, a tunneling of awareness. A balanced head, by aiming the eyes more or less at the horizon, opens up peripheral vision.

Carol was accustomed to walking with her head low-ered, eyes fixed on the ground before her. When she played the piano she habitually dropped her head and fastened her eyes on her fingers. Her playing was dry, cautious, and over-practiced.

As she discovered how to balance her head comfortably and grew accustomed to letting her gaze rest out horizontally rather than downward, she was at first literally caught off balance by the horizon arcing around her on either side with its suddenly deepened perspective. One day she became aware that the opening of her visual field was somehow con-nected with an opening of her auditory field. She had become more alive to sound: she noticed a broader spectrum and was more alert to the spatial placement of sounds. Moving through the changing sound ambiance of the day, she felt as if she were walking in the midst of an ever-renewing sonic improvisation of nature and humanity. She applied this shift of perspective to her music by freeing herself from a visual fixation on her hands and learning to maintain the balance of her head as she played. She directed her glance as if on the sound emanating upward and outward from the strings, every now and then briefly looking downward for a particu-lar technical maneuver.

Where her visual and auditory focus had previously been tightly set on the fingers initiating notes, she was now hear-ing not just the attack points but the entire envelope of each sound. She experienced a heartening renewal of enjoyment in playing, and this too was reflected in the sound: the tone became fuller and more varied, and there was broader scope to the playing, a sense of greater freedom and individuation.

Bilaterality and Rotation

"My head tilts to the side," "my left shoulder is higher," "my right hip sticks out," "one leg is shorter than the other."

Imbalance between the sides of the body is often noticed, because looking head-on into mirrors provides the visual experience most people have of themselves, and because ready-made clothing is bilaterally symmetrical while bodies generally are not.

Bilateral imbalance squeezes organs, disrupts muscular functioning, and brings tractions or pressures to bear on the nervous system. Scoliosis (sideways curvature of the spine), frequently diagnosed in children and often a progressively worsening condition among the aged, is one of the most commonly recognized evidences of a laterally asymmetrical tension pattern. Scoliosis is generally compensated by a pelvic shift to one side, which in turn can give rise to leg and foot problems. One leg will be positioned closer to the body's central axis and therefore bear more weight than the other. Neither leg can then function according to design, and all the joints will be subjected to abnormal stresses. The sacroiliac joint is particularly sensitive to lack of pelvic equipoise.

The balancing mechanisms of the inner ears, which monitor movement by sensing the body's relation to gravity, assume as their norm a head that is oriented to the horizontal and vertical and is centered over the axis of the body. Vision and hearing also function normally on a gravity-aligned grid. If the head (and therefore the perceptual grid) is tilted, eye muscles will constantly be correcting for the tilt, and the two eyes will not be precisely coordinated. Also, these delicate muscles, embedded as they are in the grosser musculature of the neck and head, will share in the more general imbalance of tensioning forces needed to carry the off-balance weight of the head. The jaw, hanging from its two sliding temporomandibular articulations and otherwise attached only loosely to the face and neck, is particularly vulnerable to bilaterally imbalanced muscular forces.

A closer look shows that front-to-back and side-to-side

imbalances are not separate phenomena but merely separate ways of viewing a single pattern of rotation. A right hip, for example, may not only protrude sideways but pull backward, while the left shoulder pulls forward and out to the left. The spine twists to support this counterbalancing. Many people, settling down to read or converse, characteristically wrap around themselves through a twist that puts most of their weight onto one haunch. Ellen, standing and talking with Jim, supposedly face-to-face, drops her weight almost entirely on her right leg; the left side of her body swings back a little to lean against the right, which is firmly planted in support. Her position is askew—she is pointed diagonally leftward from Jim, with her neck turned to the right to orient her face toward him. Though Jim is unlikely to notice consciously, Ellen is only partially present to him. Her eyes point one way while her trunk points another way; her attention and intention are not quite in focus.

Structural rotations represent patterns of movement. Powerful capacities for rotation are built into our musculature through the diagonal weave of many of the trunk muscles (Dart, 1950), as we have already seen in the tendency of limbs to rotate outward in response to chronic contraction in the trunk. This natural range of rotational movement often links with a self-limiting downward drag, the body shortening into contraction by spiraling in a preferred direction. The directional preference can be related to a number of factors: our right- or left-handedness, environment (the need of a violinist to turn and tilt her head to the left while lifting her right bowing arm up; the approach, always from the right, of customers to a cashier's desk), the asymmetry of organs (liver on one side, heart on the other), and the tendency of fluids to spiral in downward movement (clockwise in the northern hemisphere, as you can witness in your sink drain).

When we discover how to true ourselves so that our forward-backward alignment hangs slightly in front of the vertical, the downward twist of rotations is offset by the natural forces that lift us and affirm our symmetry. This is experienced as an organizing and unraveling counterbalance up and around our central axis which dialogues with the fleeting twists called forth by our activities.

Balance and Various Treatment Modalities

In surveying the effects of balance and imbalance on specific parts of the body, we have entered the realm of one after another treatment modality: optometry, podiatry, psychotherapy, physical therapy, and many different branches of medicine. As a more sophisticated awareness of the human response to gravity penetrates their theoretical foundations, all of these disciplines will be encouraged to take a broader, more contextual view of the local problems they deal with. When the possibility for dramatic permanent change in postural patterns becomes more broadly known, many modalities that in effect make the best of a bad situation— orthotic lifts in shoes, for example, or surgical interventions that limit mobility of the spine—will give way to, or will interact creatively with, methods that encourage changes in weight-bearing and movement behavior.

Chapter 5

In Two Nutshells

A soul is an immaterial thing. It is a principle of activity, it is an "act," a "form," an energizing principle. It is the life of the body.

Thomas Merton, *Seven Storey Mountain* (1948) 1976

You need imagination to form a notion of beauty at all, and still more to discover your ideal in an unfamiliar shape.

Joseph Conrad, *Amy Foster* (1901) 1976, 159

An analysis of structure is not the description of a state of things. The confusion of these two is a source of many misunderstandings and errors in all realms of life.

Paul Tillich, *Dynamics of Faith* 1958, 21

First Nutshell: Ideal Human Form

Anyone who undertakes or facilitates behavior change must entertain, however vaguely, some concept of an ideal form or there can be no sense of direction. Without it "we strive all the time," in Proust's words, "to give our life its form, but we do so by copying willy-nilly, like a drawing, the features of the person we are and not of the person we should like to be."

Ideals of the human form operate powerfully in our lives. Those who want to lead us construct models for us to emulate; great industries—cosmetics, clothing, alcohol, religion, tobacco, medicine, politics, universities—bombard us with images of the human being in order to draw us into their orbit and make customers, devotees, or students of us, saying in effect, "This is what a real human being is. Conform to this model or you'll be sorry."

Even more pervasive than commercial exploitation is the unconscious imprinting of parents' behavior, which sets up patterns of imitation that may last a lifetime and be passed along from generation to generation. Alice Miller has studied the way children who suffer parental harshness, usually justified in the interest of obedience, good manners, and discipline, express as adults a renewed outcropping of that same harshness, sometimes—as in the case of Adolph Hitler—amplified into extreme violence (Miller, 1983).

No less are we imprinted by our parents' patterns of movement: their walks, their familiar ways of standing or sitting, their head cocks and facial expressions as they chat. As we unknowingly absorb some of these we may also draw into ourselves the cynical, defensive, beaten-by-life, or arrogant attitudes these movements can reflect. In repetition after repetition they deepen their control until they seem to express who we are. We have lost some of our inborn potential to explore and establish our own, perhaps quite different, expression of life. We are a chip off the old block.

We usually embrace such patterns unconsciously. We

can disentangle ourselves from them consciously if we have a clear direction of travel—an ideal. In the realm of movement education, different disciplines espouse varying ideals, and it behooves one to ask carefully what model is under pursuit and whether its attainment is what one really wishes. A weight lifter and a gymnast may begin with a common dedication to athletic prowess, but by the time their training has specialized them, they have developed their particular genetic endowments in such radically different directions as to make them almost seem to belong to separate species.

This book presents an ideal broad enough to serve lawyer or gardener, gymnast or weight-lifter in their specific realms. The ideal form will be sketched now with broad strokes to provide a context for the principles and suggestions discussed elsewhere in more detail. You can determine the extent to which this form matches your own aspirations.

In motion or at rest, the person is peaceful, manifesting a quality of harmony that underlies the most vigorous and challenging activity. Peace is expressed in the physical structure as a release of weight onto balanced support, an integration of the body into the field of gravity. The left side balances the right, the front balances the back.

The center of gravity is high; that is, the body is vertically expansive so that its weight is poised, ready to fall into movement in any direction rather than needing to be lifted into action. The feet will, in standing, spontaneously be close to one another, contributing to this unstable and mobile system. The spinal curves are shallow—not in a swayback or "widow's hump." The head floats in easy balance on top of the spine.

The musculature of a balanced, peaceful person is mobilized for action; it is not in a state of sustained overcontraction, or "tension," which tends to pull the body in on itself, cramping joints and restricting movement. Muscular effort is appropriate to the need.

This poised person is flexible. Since no chronic muscular tension is holding joints rigid, movement flows reverberatively through the whole structure. The capacity to shift direction, physically and psychologically, is readily accessible when called for.

An easy physical presence reflects a value structure and a sense of the world in which the boundaries between self and other are rather fluid and where there is a minimal need (less than is customary in our culture) for defining oneself over-sharply and defending that definition.

The body, and more generally the person, is able to focus energy effectively—partly because there are no extraneous tensions dragging and restricting the system, partly because flexibility allows the parts of the body to be continually finding their optimal relationships. The shoulder girdle, including arms and hands, is used for delicate and discriminating action; the pelvic girdle, including legs and feet, is used for power. When heavy furniture needs to be pushed across the room, for example, the body is mobilized to bring the power of the large leg muscles to bear on the task without undue strain on the back or shoulders.

Movement invigorates. Simple daily actions (walking, reaching, bending) as well as actions which require developed skills (classical guitar playing, pole-vaulting) are gratifying and enlivening. They challenge the system to respond inventively and as a totality to immediate specific demands.

Movement in such a person is effectively characterized and not inhibited by self-consciousness. In speaking, the voice makes free use of its potential for melodic inflection and has a rich palette of rhythms and resonances. A reach outward of the arms in joyous welcome receives its entire expressive shaping. No less clear is an outward reach whose message is more complex: cheerful welcome of a friend, say, qualified by concern over her apparent low spirits. The effectiveness of skilled actions, as in a basketball player's jump shot or a cellist's bowed legato, reveals itself in the beauty of the movement shapes themselves.

Ideally, movements are articulately phrased. An action such as walking to close the door has a clear beginning, middle, and end. The meaning, or motivation, reveals itself incrementally throughout, becoming fully focused at the climax: Juan, interrupted by the noise of the neighbors across the hall, abruptly turns, strides toward the door and tosses it shut. Each of the nested subphrases (the initial turn, the separate strides, the climactic toss of the door, the impact of closing and latching, its quieting as Juan also comes to rest)— all these parts specify and yet bind themselves to the coherence of the whole phrase, and they express Juan with precision. The temporal shaping of phrase so that its component parts fall into just the right places at the right moments is, like the ocean, "tidy." Great athletes and comedians are masters of discriminative pacing, and we all have a taste for its pleasures.

Organic adeptness in activity bespeaks generosity. Each movement goes out from center and returns to center, shaping its travels in detail so that it leaves its mark in the world, and also in the person as a further enrichment of character. Such expressive and rhythmic elements of movement are not something separate from balance, poise, and flexibility.

The improvement of all these elements might seem to demand an enormously complex discipline for which only professional movement experts could find time and energy, but they are the ingredients of anyone's activity. For better or for worse, we cannot escape them, and we practice them in every move we make; they are basic ways in which we express our attitudes and cares. Reaching for a cup on the shelf or opening a door, touching others, playing racquetball—these are opportunities for bringing perceptiveness to bear on the impulses of our particular lives, and for living with more grace.

Another Nutshell: Educating Movement

"We think of artists as the expressive ones. Yet all of us, all the time, are revealing who we are and what we care about and how we make sense of the world. Movement is the medium of our inevitable expressiveness. When we open the car door, turn on a light switch, shake hands, or lift a fork we embody our delight, anger, or distractedness."

Thomas looked around at his audience, the Professionals' Club, most of whom had finished their lunch. "I am using the word *movement* broadly, in a sense that includes posture, breathing, and speaking. If you were to become aware, right at this moment, of the fact that your sitting has a style, that it is saying something to me, to others, and yourself about the way you are feeling, how would you understand its statement?"

A nervous laugh rippled across the room, with a rustle of shifting bodies. At the beginning of his talk Thomas had encouraged his audience to interrupt him with questions, and now Jim Summers, a lawyer friend sitting near the front, spoke up.

"Why do you think your question made us self-conscious? Nearly everybody straightened up."

Seeing a thoughtful smile on a young woman in the corner, Thomas invited her response. "My posture was not expressing my state of mind very well," she said. "I was slouched down and probably looked bored, but actually I was following you with interest." She reflected a moment. "I work almost every day in planning sessions. I wonder if this drooped way of sitting hides my real dedication."

Jim commented again. "I was taught that posture was important in making a good impression. When you asked about sitting, my response was to shape up. It was almost a reflex, and happened before I had even noticed what my posture was."

A woman beside Jim spoke, almost in irritation. "Wouldn't it be better not to call attention to posture? Isn't it more honest to be who we are, slouched or whatever, and not force ourselves to maintain a pose to impress someone?"

"*Who we are* is just the question," answered Thomas. "Every time we move we reveal ourselves. But is it our true self, acting in response to this very moment, or is it an automatic and habit-ridden self?

"Do you remember how intensely you felt things in childhood—the atmosphere of the kindergarten room, your parents arguing in the car, your dog dying? Childhood experiences imprint deeply, on bodies as well as spirits. We may absorb posture from parents without ever realizing it, or unknowingly imitate present models—a boss or a wife or an aunt. But these borrowings are not who we are.

"We can take conscious steps to discover movement that is more natural to us and respects our dynamic architecture. Not just for an impression we can create, although no doubt we will look more assured, flexible, and graceful, but for an appearance that is authentic, that reflects us truthfully."

A woman in the back said, "Could you give us an example from your personal experience? Why did you get involved with this work?"

"I was a violinist. After years of intense practicing I began to realize that certain self-limiting habits, part of my basic style of personal behavior, were in control of my music-making. Recitals filled me with stage fright. I couldn't bring into performance the nuance or vividness I was feeling in the music. My inspiration, denied expression, was not growing. I was getting in my own way.

"But how could I shift my approach and remedy these difficulties? I wondered if movement study might be a path to unabashed, impassioned expressiveness, to freedom from obsolete habits. And it was. A piece of music moves—it makes a shape in time. It also moves us, touches us. And I move to play."

As Thomas took a sip of water, an athletic-looking young man asked whether he taught a form of exercise.

"Yes and no," Thomas answered. "I do teach some formalized movement processes, but their chief purpose is to suggest change in ordinary movements such as walking and sitting. There has been a wave of interest in movement education in recent years: aerobics, jogging, racquetball, yoga, and martial arts. These can increase alertness, strength, flexibility, and cardiovascular health. They can lower one's tension level and they are pleasurable.

"But they are special activities added to our usual round. Suppose we take our daily affairs themselves—their expression in movement—as a place to enjoy our natural physical state. If getting out of bed, walking downstairs, driving to work, and sitting at a desk could become more healthful and enjoyable, if they had more of the zest that we love in our games, if they could lift us up rather than just move us along or even drag us down, then the whole fabric of life would be strengthened and enriched. And this qualitative change would improve a racquetball game too, or a violin performance, or the doing of any job.

"It's easy for people to ignore the way they move. We are accustomed to leaving movement in the realm of the unconscious and letting habit take care of the details. Even those of us who depend on specialized movements for work or play may become completely unaware of them once a basic pattern of coordination is learned. Think how unconsciously you type or drive a car. Attention gets captured by what we are accomplishing, by where we are going.

"This unconsciousness about movement frees our minds from operational detail, but it can also create a problem. Because we are unaware of them, habits that we have developed in the past adhere to us, shaping present movement."

Jim interjected, "I should think the unconsciousness you mention would also keep people away from movement education. Most people just don't care. What motivates your students to come in the first place?"

"Sometimes life forces attention onto movement. If you have a painful shoulder, it makes sense to look at the way its muscles and bones are functioning in relationship to one another. Are they working as they were designed? Suppose you drop a clock on the floor and some of the shafts and wheels get out of alignment. It still runs, but it doesn't keep time very well; there are points of strain where the cogs don't quite mesh and will wear out. So-called bad posture is a similar distortion which creates points of strain. Awareness of movement can help a person to untwist, to rediscover the design. It is a simple and practical approach to many kinds of pain.

"Sometimes people come to movement education because they want to improve a skill, and they intuit that to broaden its context will help. What guitarists or dental technicians do with their hands depends on their sitting, standing, reaching, and bending; their deftness is based on this background of movement."

The woman beside Jim spoke up again. "My father nagged me about good posture. The very notion makes me uncomfortable. Do you know what I mean?"

"Sure," said Thomas. "The common image of standing up straight and sitting up straight is of something forced: put your head up, pull your shoulders back, tighten your stomach, tuck in your buttocks, then hold. It's no surprise that we rebel against this imposed and artificial exertion."

Thomas paused a moment to emphasize his words. "Balance, as an ideal, takes us in a better direction. A body in balance provides secure support for itself with no more muscular effort than is needed for present activity. Balance can be learned—it is straightforward.

"You might say that a body in balance has its skeleton in the right place to be rested on. And so another factor, the release of weight, can come into play. We rest our weight on its own skeletal support. This kind of relaxation can be part of the most vigorous activity, and it frees the body to be flexible and responsive."

Another voice spoke up. "Do you really mean that an ideal is operating here?"

"Yes," answered Thomas, "and hopefully a truer one than the ideal of stiff good posture. Instead of *ideal* we might use a more neutral word like *structure*, suggesting that there is, objectively, an inherent design to the musculoskeletal system and that when we know what it is, we can allow it to function optimally. But there is more to our design than its efficiency: there is its capacity for expressiveness. When we move, we show what we care about, where we choose to focus our energies. People with back pain may begin to see the need to examine and transform the values being expressed in their movement. For example, if a man habitually struts arrogantly, rigidifying his spine, this way of identifying himself may lie behind the tension that generates the pain. The word *ideal* incorporates a quality of aspiration for happiness, perhaps for more ethical behavior, for a dimension that is deeper than the mechanics of balance.

"We all know people who are chronically anxious, who shrink back from what they encounter in life. Most of us have a share of this so-called state anxiety. The emotional tendency, the habit, is expressed in movement, and here the word *posture* is appropriate because a held emotion will show up as a holding of the body. Anxiety, for example, is likely to take up residence in us as a chronic pulling up and forward of shoulders and a depression of ribs. The pattern of tension takes the body off its natural balance—the rib cage, say, is not only depressed but settles back, behind its pelvic support, and the head thrusts forward; to maintain its uprightness, the body must fight a gravitational drag.

"This off-balanced physical state is felt as anxiety. And so we have a vicious circle: imbalance expresses anxious tension, which induces greater imbalance, which expresses greater anxious tension, and so forth. The aging process is often caught up in a circle which gives gravity a more and more destructive pull on us. Awareness of movement is a way of reversing the direction of travel around the circle: improved balance expresses greater peace and confidence; these induce yet more refined balance, and so forth."

A woman interrupted musingly. "Can we go back for a minute? You suggested that our movement reveals a choice of values. Are you implying that if we are angry or anxious or have a painful shoulder, this is by choice?"

"Perhaps *choice* is the wrong word. Imbalance generally starts in childhood and may never be very conscious. But it is choice in the sense that most people could, with sufficient understanding and motivation, make a shift."

"I've had low back pain for eight years," said the woman. "It began with a car accident. Do you think I could heal this myself? The doctors have given up on me."

"Movement education would certainly be worth a try," answered Thomas. "You can learn a more efficient, less stressful use of your back. And by developing perceptivity, not just of the pain but of your back's capacity for support and movement even in its present state, you may learn to release an overprotective contraction that interferes with healing."

A question came from an older man who was obviously sitting, somewhat uncomfortably, more erect than was usual for him. "I've been experimenting with posture during your talk, and it strikes me that overcoming a habit I've practiced for sixty-five years is too demanding. If I don't keep my attention on it I forget, and my old posture comes back immediately. I'm writing a book that takes close concentration. I can see that better balance and release of tension might improve my health and even give me more energy, but splitting my attention seems too costly."

"It's a good idea," answered Thomas, "to understand from the beginning that the refashioning of movement calls for commitment. Persistence and patience are two main ingredients. But movement awareness needn't be a constant distraction. It can operate pointedly, like the attention you give to your book; it can also function in a less focused way, as a background of perceptions. *Presence* is a good word for this diffuse awareness, and it is a natural capability.

"I encourage my students to spend a little time each day giving their full attention to movement behavior. As I mentioned, I often teach formal exercises to music. These are processes that familiarize them with specific aspects of movement, such as balance in standing or arm weight in reaching.

The rest of the day they are encouraged to let these lessons play a supportive but less focused role in the midst of their normal activities.

"If one maintains presence while applying more specific principles of sitting, standing, reaching, and bending, the work continues to deepen; it becomes an ongoing exploration with focused attention flowing in and out of it. Taken in this spirit, movement study could enhance concentration on your book."

A comment came from a woman who had been listening intently. "In the theater the word *presence* refers to personal magnetism. I've been directing the Community Players and am bothered by the cluttered gestures and hurried manner of my actors. How would movement study help their stage presence?"

"That brings up the subject of phrasing," Thomas answered. "Whether for actors, musicians, dancers, or speakers, stage presence depends on sharply delineating what is happening at each moment. We communicate clearly by shaping units that are distinct yet flow from one to the next: like a breath, each act, each scene or sentence has a beginning, reaches a climax, concludes, rests, and then flows into the next action. As you are aware, much of your work as a director is to clarify the phrasing of the play itself into meaningful divisions.

"The detailed shaping of phrase happens in the performer's movement—including, of course, the speaking. I found out in violin playing that a musical phrase isn't shaped just by the arms, hands, and fingers but also by the swaying and nodding movements of trunk and head. If those movements are poorly formed, if they do not suit the laws of motion that are inherent in the body's structure, the phrases will sound ill–timed and lack fullness. The movements will contradict rather than express the shape of the music. It's no different for an actor.

"And the same line of approach applies to the movements of daily life. What better words can we use than *cluttered* and *hurried* to describe the general malaise of our culture? Your actors are expressing this quality not just on stage but throughout their lives. Awareness directed to the phrasing of their movement will not only improve their performance in the play but lift them to a more zestful and peaceful level through the rest of the day."

Thomas summarized. "If I were to give a name to the movement ideal that expresses our basic human nature, I would call it 'generosity.' Generous movement is a healthy and happy expression of the structure we humans were born with; it has clarity, breadth, and refinement, the capacity for strong outgoing action and for delicate sensitivity. Generous movement reflects a generous spirit, and expanding our awareness of movement can be a path to opening ourselves in both realms."

Chapter 6

Percipience

More than erect on her chair she flung her head nobly backwards, for, while always a great lady, she was a trifle inclined to act the part of the great lady too.
Marcel Proust, *Remembrance of Things Past* (1913–1927) 1981, II: 544

A weird life it is, indeed, to be living always in somebody else's imagination, as if it were the only place in which one could at last become real!
Thomas Merton, *Seven Storey Mountain* (1948) 1976

The Destructiveness of Ideals

There are snares in ideals that may limit their usefulness to us, and may in fact make them deleterious. The impulse to be correct, to do it right, to conform to an abstraction, may lead not to a flexible extension of one's range but to discouragement and to recoiling from one's natural capacities. The ideal of the 20-year-old athlete or model, reaching out from TV commercials, movies, and magazines to entice us, no matter what our own God-given proportions, may serve as a Procrustean bed where we beat ourselves with hammers if we are too short and cut off our legs if we are too long. Put a mirror in front of a student in a movement session in order to observe some particular quality of movement (how the right leg swings out or the knee turns in) and you will most likely evoke not awareness but irrelevant dismay: "I'm too fat, too bony, my teeth aren't straight, my hair is thin." Inappropriate or impossible ideals ("If only I were three inches taller") can exert insidious power over our lives, and even those ideals that are perhaps appropriate (the 200 pounds that "should be" 165 pounds) often seem to function as a source of humiliation that perpetuates the problem rather than solving it.

Bob Kriegel's process in learning to ski illustrates a snare frequently lying in wait for those who seek to follow an ideal: the tendency to ignore actual experience.

> When I was a beginner, the "correct" way to ski was to keep your legs tightly pressed together with your boots touching. . . . All my efforts were guided by this concept of how I *should* be skiing, and I never focused on how my body responded to it or whether it actually worked for me or not. At first it felt uncomfortable and unnatural. But I wasn't concerned with how my body was feeling because I wanted so badly to do it *right*. (Gallwey and Kriegel 1977, 37)

The power of "should" blinded Kriegel to "is": it cut off his resources for exploring and enjoying his own present experience of skiing and for learning from his experience. The attachment to what is right gives rise to self-consciousness; it organizes personal energies around an idea, and a more spontaneous upwelling of impulse is suppressed. The awkwardness of Kriegel's learning process as he saw it in hindsight lay partly in the arbitrariness of the model he was imitating, but even more in his trying to swallow it whole. The ideal sat inside him, unassimilated, like the elephant swallowed by the snake in *The Little Prince*.

As an example of people trapped by an inappropriate ideal, George Dennison, in *The Lives of Children* (1969), describes two baseball games going on at different ends of the same field. One game is full of laughter, dogs, grass, and improvisation out of momentary impulse. The other is made up of uniforms, rules, the urgent cries of stern-faced daddies with a passion for victory. Here the children conform to an adult image; they measure themselves against an ideal and see themselves, their activity, in its light.

In stage fright, anxiety arises from the contrast between ideal and self and from the impulse to conceal one's own inadequacies. Performance under such circumstances is less likely to be a mode of self-expression, the sharing of one's actual resources, skills, and inspiration, than an attempt to deliver a product which has already been defined and to which we attempt to measure up. The problem is not in being a "perfectionist"—we all admire people who pursue goals until they reach extraordinary levels of skill—but in relating to an ideal in such a way that the learning process is stifled by it rather than given breath.

Self-Confirmation

The relationship with ideals may readily be blighted and undependable when perceptiveness of self or environment is faulty. Many of us keep constant company with a low-grade uneasy self-consciousness. It is present through most of our undertakings so that we are not quite at home with actions and interactions. We may put on airs or be pettily secretive, even false, though we wish to be spontaneously direct. These posturings cling to us and form an incrustation which separates us from discernment of our internal and external worlds and from a supple response. Thomas Hora's term *self-confirmation* is suggestive in describing this nearly universal mode of self-consciousness (Hora, *Existential Metapsychiatry*, 1977).

One of the qualities of self-confirmation is narcissism. The self becomes fascinated with its echoes and reflections in the world, and even more with its own reaction to the supposed impressions it is making. This emotional response, an exaggerated attraction to or repulsion from self-image, fixates attention. Janie's sulking gives her a sharp flavorful experience: it burns and it stimulates a steady flow of psychic activity. She is not a nobody.

The development of self-confirmation is a loss of innocence. The most important knowledge that Adam and Eve acquired from the serpent was a sense of the reflected self: "they knew that they were naked," that someone was looking at them and that their nakedness was an intolerably direct expression of themselves. They forthwith put on fig leaves, "and hid themselves from the presence of the Lord God" (Genesis 3:8).

Recoil, the contraction of muscles into habitual expressive postures, is a physical strategy of self–confirmation, a fig leaf in the flesh, a hardening of tissue into an identity that masks our rich potential. In rigidifying the body, recoil creates internal friction, a constant reminder of one's existence. Janie's sulking, by tightening her rib cage, makes inhalation more difficult, and because it must push against resistance, it is felt more strongly. She will carry some of this pattern of restriction with her when she goes out to play. In its tendency to pull her ribs down and her shoulders up and forward, it will create over time a recognizable posture, an identity which has her style of response built into it. As Janie practices sulking, she channels herself more and more deeply into this particular form of self-knowledge and loses the capacity for spontaneous expression. Also she diminishes the capacity to be rescued from her habit-worn responses by an ideal external to them; rather, she will be inclined to misconstrue the ideal and to respond to it from her narrowed groove of already established routines and reactions.

Habits of self-confirmation are deeply ingrained. They are learned in childhood and are often assumed to be natural. Through the familiar process of introjection—incorporating images of the environment into the psyche (and the body) and experiencing them as oneself—we identify with the social ocean in which we swim.

Charlie, in the fifth grade, was a little slow in his physical maturation, certainly not up to the level of three or four boys and girls in his class whose musculature and nervous systems had already developed into athletic prowess. On the playground these stars did most of the running, tagging, and throwing while Charlie and the others were pulled here and there by the current of more focused energy. What was impressed upon Charlie by this powerful course in physical education was that he, in contrast with the ideal held up to him by his precocious classmates, was clumsy and ineffective in his movements. Charlie's father contributed his own sense of disappointment and made a moral issue of clumsiness by calling him lazy. At an earlier, more innocent stage of his development, when he was first learning to walk, Charlie was able to hold an implicit image—an ideal—of walking and to strive intensely toward it, suffering falls and frustrations in plenty without setting them into his system. But in the fifth grade he was disgusted and frightened by the discovery of his supposed inferiority and, like Janie, fixed an idea of himself in relation to others and began to shape his life to fit. Forty years later Charlie still feels dismayed by his movement behavior. Many choices—career, marriage, recreation—have been decisively steered by his sense of inadequacy, and these later choices have of course provided ongoing reinforcement for his patterns.

Charlie's behavior is self-confirming in that the identity he fabricated in childhood goes on developing and polishing and perfecting itself. One of the potent tools of this process is projection. As he more and more assumes that others see him the way he sees himself, he is of course more and more correct; his sense of being awkward tends to make him so. Social dancing has always been a painful experience because his awkwardness has seemed to be on display, and the sarcastic contempt he has developed for athletes and dancers as mindless boors is in part a defense against the scorn he expects from them.

We people the world with our projections. Those who are trigger-happy with their anger know that the world is full of irritating people and situations. When Gerald says that a stoplight is frustrating, the frustration seems to be in the light, not in his reaction; when Amy recoils into anxiety, the curtness of her landlord's voice on the telephone, which yesterday seemed to be because he wanted to get back to the baseball game, now sounds like anger over the broken window; she worries that he will evict her and she will have to go back to Cincinnati and live with mother, and so on. Amy is not only the leading puppet in this drama but the puppeteer and playwright as well, as is easy for bystanders to see unless they have been drawn into supporting roles.

Self-confirmation is a merry-go-round combination of projection and introjection. I project what I introject, and I introject what I project, a tissue of fabrications that weaves back and forth between "inside" and "outside." The distinction between myself and not-myself is part of the fabrication. It increases, with each new strand, my aloneness. And yet at the same time this isolated "I" is more and more firmly bound into that marketplace of interactions. I have a position, a precarious security.

Anxiety, one by-product of self-confirmation, is often the free-floating, background sort which can attach itself to any momentary situation as a supposed cause. The carefully assembled personality senses that its troops are all on the front line; it is constantly defending what it doesn't have much faith in, what it knows little about because its attention has been so fixed on how it looks to others and on how it feels about that. "And doubtless," says Rilke, "the ingenious animals notice that we're not so reliably at home in our interpreted world" (*First Duino Elegy* [1923] 1989).

Ideals in general, and ideals of the human being in particular, lend themselves to the service of self-confirmation by providing an abstraction against which actuality is judged. The concept of an ideal "me" provides an endlessly serviceable device for bringing attention to bear on my faults. From the viewpoint of the isolated self, struggling to establish its illusory identity, self-criticism is tempting. Unpleasant as it is, it stirs feelings that indicate to me that I (the fabricated "I" of my self-confirmation) really do exist. Since parents almost universally use ideals as sticks for beating their children, it is no wonder that having introjected those parents we take up the sticks and beat ourselves with them.

The Generosity of Human Form

God, as the conceived source of goodness and happiness in life, exists in some traditions as an ideal of perfection whose life and being are totally separate from ours. He lives elsewhere, in heaven, a place which contains the qualities that our world lacks. This God and this heaven can readily function as agents of self-confirmation. We cannot penetrate that world, it does not penetrate us except to make adverse judgments; we are over against it, we relate to it, our surfaces strike against its surfaces. If an intermediary like Jesus or an enemy like Satan are in the picture, they too may be seen as totally magnificent others; against their images our own plays in contrast.

One alternative is to see God not as something other but as the most essential quality of our own being, our ground or core. "Self" is then not a ricocheting billiard ball in a world of discrete objects, one of which is God. Self is the manifestation, or expression, of God. God is the substratum, the principle or ideal of each person's selfness. Our essential nature is to manifest the life that rises up in us, to be expressive, or creative. And since that life is already structured, prior to or deeper than the "us" of our consciousness, our creativity is a process of discovery, of uncovering and characterizing what is there.

The degree to which consciousness remains true to this structure is (since the structure is oneself) the measure of our authenticity. Self-confirmation, in separating consciousness from its grounding, turns it to the service of faking and masking, of fashioning a structure out of the litter of impressions that arise in the separation. The aliveness that undergirds us is also the ground of the living things around us and of inanimate things. Rivers, foxes, trees, and buildings are shaped by the same laws of form that shape humans.

> The force that through the green fuse drives the flower
> Drives my green age; that blasts the roots of trees
> Is my destroyer. (Dylan Thomas 1957, 10)

As the science of ecology and the bitter experience of pollution are teaching us, "self" has no sharp boundaries but is a node of energy in a great field where nothing occurs anywhere without occurring everywhere. The structure that we manifest is neither "inside" nor "outside." From the understanding of this unity flows the set of values (including values related to the body) which are true to our nature and therefore can lead us toward happiness. The word *generosity* sums up this set of values which allows us to flow more freely and sensitively with our environment. The word is particularly useful here because it can be applied to movement as well as to attitude and social action.

An ideal of human nature cannot be either accurate or functional—in the sense of providing guidance in truing our behavior to our innate form—unless it leads away from self-consciousness, away from self-confirmation and, through percipience, to generosity.

Stalking

The shift from self-consciousness to self-awareness—percipience—is a shift in the understanding of "self." Self-consciousness emphasizes identity. It focuses attention on "characteristics," distinguishing marks, personality, those aspects of self which show or which would show if we didn't hide them. Self-consciousness also includes an element of reaction, of recoil, of taking a position with respect to the experience of self. Percipience, on the other hand, brings attention to structure, to continuity, to basic nature, to the order from which behavior arises. This sense of wholeness includes a softening of the boundaries between individual and surroundings. The self, rather than being fixed in its context, is fluid enough to be continually refined and shaped by the experience it generates, to be made new by it in the moment-by-moment process of living. Percipience leads to insights about self-confirmatory behavior: as underlying structure emerges into clarity, incongruity between behavior and structure becomes clearer as well. So percipience tends to act as a solvent to inauthentic or incongruent behavior, while self-consciousness tends to reinforce it.

Percipience is not judgmental: it does not place me opposite some real or imagined being and ask me to conform to that image; it puts me in touch with myself. If an incongruity appears, it is understood as a sign of self-contradiction, of parts of myself that are not successful in manifesting my own deeper structure.

Janie's brother Gerald, now 41 years old, has been hiking alone in the mountains for several days. One of his reasons for going to the out-of-doors is, he tells himself, to become more "porous," to let the profusion of life penetrate him, here where it feels most safe to him—where he has nothing to prove, where his ordinary goals are irrelevant, where no one is watching.

And yet he finds that he is hiking as if it were important to be somewhere other than right here. He sets arbitrary goals—to climb Mt. Stanley, to reach the Cedar River—and often finds himself walking along totally absorbed in his thoughts, only vaguely aware of clouds and bushes. If he looks at the flowers, he studies them: learns their names and classifications, and spends more time attending to the botany book than to the plants. He enjoys challenging himself and proving his stamina, but knows that the issue of endurance is a secondary motive for being here.

He feels like an invader in the woods, not belonging the way squirrels and pine trees do, and unwittingly he accentuates his separateness with rigid and noisy boots that frighten the animals and crush the plants, with his campfires, his tent, his food, even his sleeping bag.

Gerald is competent in handling practical matters, and this evening he has busied himself with setting up camp. Realizing that he has not seen any deer on this entire trip, he walks out into the dusk to look for them. But no amount of wishing or of managerial competence will materialize a deer to his view. While he moves through the meadow a shift of consciousness gradually occurs, as if by grace: forgetting about the gritty determination to see deer, he is suffused by a receptivity to the sounds and shapes of dusk which are presenting themselves to him, and he gives himself over to a rapt appreciation. Continuing to stroll, he becomes aware that what has drawn him to the wilderness is to find and to exercise just this attitude of stalking: a global alertness, open to sound or sight anywhere around him, mirrored by an inner quiet. His stalking is more than a heightening of sensory antennae and a quieting of mental bustle. It is a shift of physical being: his movement is awakened and supple, with a flamboyance just beneath the surface, even while the contact of his footsteps and his brushing against shrubs has become more finely attuned. Gerald stalks the deer, the wilderness, and himself for 10 or 15 minutes before he wanders again into a labyrinth of thoughts and fantasies. The experience remains a touchstone, however, part of the ideal he holds of his authentic self.

Over the years Gerald had "tried" meditation a number of times and "failed" because he was discouraged by the continuing onward rush of his thoughts. Stalking gives him a new insight into the possibility and the value of meditation for him: it is not simply an inward journey, not just an attempt to discipline his unruly mind, but an evocation of the state of presence, of belonging in the very time and place he finds himself, thoughts included. Here is just the porous quality he was looking for in the mountains.

Sensory Perception

The favor of grace on this wilderness occasion had bathed Gerald with percipience. How can he build on this experience—deliberately evoke and maintain percipience as a significant attribute of his consciousness? How can he avoid the ever-ready pitfalls of self-consciousness and self-confirmation? There are innumerable approaches to developing "mindfulness." Time-honored among these, and practiced in many religious disciplines of meditation and prayer all over the world, is to attend to one's own breathing. Perception is focused on an immediacy of experience, on simply noticing the ebb and flow of the breath without interfering with it: along the exhalation to a pause, into the inhalation, reaching a peak, and then turning around into exhalation. The self-conscious "I" diminishes in the presence of the simple reality of breath, and the more focused the perception of breath becomes, the more awakened is sensing in general.

When awareness is allowed to focus on breathing, without manipulation, the balance of higher (cerebral) and lower (reflexive) levels of the nervous system shifts. The higher level (consciousness), responding to the reflexive level (spontaneous breathing), releases some of its interference—which is, at least in part, what we have described as self-consciousness or self-confirmation. Emotionally and mentally, this is a quieting; physiologically, it manifests as smoother and more effective movement. Watch people as they bring their attention (but not conscious control) to their breathing, and you will characteristically see rib movements become fuller, freer, and rhythmically more even, as if obstructions were being removed.

Thomas was developing his students' capacity for sensing when he had them focus on the release of the weight of an arm or leg into a partner's hands. Through perception of what was there (the actuality of the weight of their own arm, their own leg) they began to recognize what was not there (the weight that was withheld by chronic tension). Biofeedback works similarly. By observing the readout of instruments measuring such physical states as the temperature of the hand or the activity of forehead muscles, one perceives what normally is unnoticed and can learn voluntary control over factors contributing to high blood pressure, migraine headaches, and other supposedly involuntary processes.

"Sensing" has been explored in depth as a discipline called sensory awareness, originating in Germany with Elsa Gindler in the first part of the 20th century and developed in this country under the leadership of Charlotte Selver. The study of sensory awareness brings attention to sensation (touching, seeing, hearing), without a burdensome overlay of mental manipulation. As Charles Brooks, Charlotte Selver's collaborator, has said,

> Like Hamlet's, our world has become sicklied with thought. We do not refer to our own experience but to our overwhelming legacy of the conceptualizations of others. . . . If our actions derive ultimately from our beliefs—i.e. our *concepts*—we are forever manipulating a world we do not directly perceive and therefore cannot know. . . . The study of this work is our whole organismic functioning in the world we perceive. . . . We aim to discover what is natural in this functioning and what is conditioned: what is our nature, which evolution has designed to keep us in touch with the rest of the world,

> and what has become our "second nature," as Charlotte
> likes to call it, which tends to keep us apart. (Brooks
> 1978, 6–7, 17)

A sensory awareness workshop consists of situations in which you are encouraged simply to keep attention focused on sensations: the feel of a stone resting on your forehead, for example, or of your feet walking across a carpet. The sensations chosen are the kinds that we process all the time but to which we seldom or never give our concentrated, conscious attention. When we do, a remarkable quieting and sense of well-being are likely to occur. Focusing awareness is not in itself the goal but a means for regaining presence to oneself and the environment, a presence that is impaired by a life lived from idea to idea.

Those who develop a taste for sensory awareness find that it becomes an ongoing dimension of their life—that their attention can play in and out of "sensing" throughout the day, quieting and integrating them when they move their focus into it and leaving a residue of well-being when the focus moves elsewhere. The development of the capacity for sensory awareness can continue indefinitely as a part of ordinary activity, leading one deeper year by year. Our appreciation of the simple givens of life, the taken-for-granted elements such as breathing, light, color, textures, the contours of things, and the kinesthetic feel of one's own movement, is progressively enhanced.

Vivid perception stimulates thinking, which can fold back into the perception, enriching it; but the thinking easily slips aside, dissociates itself from the perception, and reverts to the spin of catch truisms by which we codify and subvocalize experience. Charlie, as if for the first time, becomes aware of the sensation of a piece of watermelon in his hands; he is amazed by its coolness, by the smoothness of its rind, and the rough sponginess of the fruity portion. Almost instanta-

neously these refreshing perceptions are submerged by a dis-
mayingly hackneyed rhapsody of thoughts: "Why haven't I
noticed this sooner? Never used to even like watermelon . . .
til I was fourteen, that picnic at Fordham. . . . I never notice
things. . . . That's what my father always told me. . . . Who's
he to blame me? Probably why the cup broke the other day; it
was already cracked, I just didn't notice. . . . It's just like the
time. . . ."

For its conceptual significance to emerge, sensory perception needs to be dwelt upon. The cellist Piatagorsky used
to encourage his students to "linger on the long notes" and
respond to their own instinct to live deep within the sound.

Apropos of sustaining a perception and increasing its
reality rather than letting it become an excuse for gratuitous
fantasy, an approach offered by Thomas Hora can be helpful.
If we are sad or have a headache, our tendency is to look for
an explanation, to ask why. Hora suggests that this question
be replaced by a search for meaning (*Existential Metapsychiatry*
1977; see also Gendlin 1981 and Ziegler 1983). The perceptual
experience can then yield insight into operational values, because personality, constructed by self-confirmatory behavior,
means something by its actions, including its perceptions,
and is always asserting its identity, its thought and feeling of
itself. One value of perception is that it provides a perspective
different from that of the personality, an independent ground
from which to observe personality itself.

If Janie, now 35 years old, notices that she has a headache and is inclined not simply to regard herself as its victim
but in some way as its generator, the question "Why do I
have a headache" will probably bring up endless answers
from within the mythology of her identity: Charlie was mean
to her this morning, the smog is bad for her sinuses, she
drank too much cognac last night, her parents were divorced

when she was little. The statements may be true, but they do not put her in possession of factors that lead to a resolution because they assume as their *modus operandi* the very self that has created the headache. If, on the other hand, she asks for the meaning of the headache, she is asking what her values are and in what way they manifest as malaise. She is looking for a different perspective from which to view her own behavior, an avenue for at least part of herself to step back and see things differently.

Janie puts herself into a free-floating state of consciousness while asking what she means by having a headache. Charlie was in fact cross with her this morning, and she has a strong suspicion that her headache is a response. The word *control* floats across her mind; it isn't quite right but there is a ring of truth: Charlie's ill-temper was not the last word. The headache will be. She is manipulating the situation. Janie flushes with chagrin as a more accurate phrase surfaces: "Paying him back!" She is up to her old trick of punishing others by hurting herself. And along with the operational value she can sense much more clearly how she expresses her desire for revenge in the tension of her neck, shoulders, and face, a pattern in which the headache participates. Janie's answer invites her to shift values: to understand herself and Charlie differently and to behave in the light of that understanding.

In the meantime, how has the headache fared? By not tamping it down into mere symptom, by viewing it from a more inclusive perspective, she has freed the headache to come under closer observation. She senses the headache, with empathy, and in detail: not just as the "usual headache." As she is in the act of perceiving, the pain becomes clearer—its location and qualities of pressure and throb more specific. Perhaps it begins to ease away, perhaps not; in either case she has been doing healing work.

Percipience is both sustained attentiveness to sensory experience and the derivation of meaning from that experience. Percipience invites us to reach through self-confirming behavior and habitual assumptions toward accuracy of observation. As nuanced experience becomes telling to us, we respond as if we hear. An ideal then is able to educate us. We can measure and mold our form by the light of its form, even as we sense its form to be malleable and evolving.

A Brief Digression on Cause-and-Effect Thinking

It is worth noting how our language tempts one into cause-and-effect thinking about the relationship of forces. Sagging of the rib cage does not cause an imbalance of the shoulder girdle any more than imbalance causes sagging; emotional depression does not cause the physical manifestation, nor is the reverse true. These factors are interactive: together they are the situation. One or another may be more accessible to our deliberate intention to change—indeed, we are suggesting that movement be given attention because it often yields readily. But this is not the same thing as causation.

Causal thinking is misleading in part because it disrupts the process of contextualizing. If I say, "This pain in my shoulder is caused by contraction of the deltoid muscle," I may have discovered something significant, but I am encouraged by the verbal form not to look further; if I say, "This pain in my shoulder and this contraction of the deltoid muscle are parts of the same situation," I am impelled to ask further: "What is this 'situation'?" And that question about the larger dimensions, the context, may lead to change.

Causal thinking is a next-door neighbor to blaming. It is an easy slide from "when my work piles up my shoulders get tense," to "shoulder tension runs in my family." The first statement makes a potentially useful observation by bringing related factors together; the second takes attention away from one important and changeable element in the situation, my reaction pattern, and places it where I probably have the least leverage and where my helplessness is emphasized.

The causal and fault-finding logic of the legal system sometimes discourages healing of injuries when a lucrative insurance settlement is to be lost by recovery.

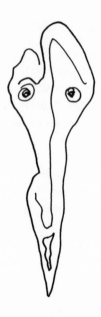

Chapter 7

Self-Determination

. . . habit is, of all the plants of human growth, the one
that has least need of nutritious soil in order to live,
and is the first to appear on the most seemingly barren
rock. . . .

Marcel Proust, *Remembrance of Things Past*
(1913–1927) 1981, II: 123

Alienating the Familiar

Only accidental bits of stuff like the earth, floating in momentary equilibrium between extremes of cold and heat, permit
such a fragile unlikelihood as life. From the perspective of
recoil we see ourselves striving endlessly and hopelessly
against a universe that is out of scale with our modest proportions. Self-confirmation and recoil are practically life itself,
our moment by moment barricade against the tremendous
forces that will overcome us, today or tomorrow.

> "He's still alive," said Bianchon.
> "And what does it get him?" asked Sylvie.
> "Suffering," said Eugène. (Balzac, *Père Goriot* [1834] 1950, 281)

And yet. And yet. Without wiping away the desperate sense of our fragility, life also speaks in a different voice. There is a happy expressiveness, an ease and fluency that is a natural birthright.

If we look just commonsensically at the way the human body's balance and movement have evolved, the conclusion seems obvious that we are not made for sustained recoil, and that an understanding of our physical architecture points toward a particular realm of values: at the spiritual level coming to friendlier terms with the universe as it is; at the psychological level releasing neurotic self–centeredness into a more flowing generosity; and at the physical level regaining balanced, reverberative movement.

Without having fathomed the mystery of Job—how a world so full of suffering can be a manifestation of goodness—an intelligent choice in playing the cards dealt to us is to act as if the universe might be a kinder and more nurturing place than inherited habits of mind have led us to believe. We have enough experience of projection to know that when attitudes change, the world changes; we don't need to find ultimate answers to ultimate questions before taking practical steps to sweeten our living space by taking responsibility for our habitual approach to the world. And those steps might also make the overall picture clearer to us.

Changing basic habits, the sort that we learned in childhood and that have embedded themselves in our movements, takes a willingness to apply attention and energy in a particular direction over a period of time. The sense of direction is established by an ideal, an image toward which one moves. The ideal functions best not as a model to be imitated but as a challenge to established patterns, a source for questioning and exploration. An ideal in this sense can stimulate many repeated moments of percipience, those glimmerings that break up the unconsciousness of habit and establish, at least momentarily, a new standpoint from which to understand and feel ourselves and our world.

If the ideal is operating as a model for imitation ("you should always walk with your spine straight," "you should be nice to your brother"), those precious moments of percipience will probably be thrown away. The contrast between model and self will capture attention, stimulating a reaction of disappointment, humiliation, or rebellion—emotions of recoil that deflect awareness from the behavior in question and fix it in the reaction. If a deliberate act of imitation follows (straightening up), attention will be focused largely on the ideal, as with Bob Kriegel learning to ski. The new behavior will remain foreign, an act of conformity, an assumption.

On the other hand, when the ideal operates as a new vantage point rather than as a model it can draw attention to what has been unconscious. This attitude is very like scientific detachment, what Bertolt Brecht called "alienating the familiar."

> To transform himself from general passive acceptance to a corresponding state of suspicious inquiry he would need to develop that detached eye with which the great Galileo observed a swinging chandelier. He was amazed by this pendulum motion, as if he had not expected it and could not understand its occurring, and this enabled him to come on the rules by which it was governed. (Brecht [1947–1948] 1964, 192)

Ideal Form as a Guide

Habits that pervade the onward flow of life are likely to be transformed in many increments of enlightenment, small steps which suffuse what is familiar and often unconscious about ourselves with a new perspective of awareness. ("I've never noticed how I lock my knees and tighten the back of my legs when I wash the dishes.") These crucial opportunities for perception are golden moments, not to be wasted.

When we follow the impulse to allow movement behavior to be expressive of our true, "ideal" self, we may be obstructed by the overlay of less appropriate movement which has become our style and which now seems natural. Habituated walking, sitting, and reaching form an unconscious standard—what F. M. Alexander called "debauched kinesthesia." It may take a mirror to convince Jonathan that when he feels as though he is standing tall his head is still cocked to the right.

We can reach through habit to recollect the truly natural. One way is to abstract, simplify, and refine a few movements which lie behind the multiplicity of the day's actions—standing, sitting, reaching, bending, walking—in order to clarify our understanding of the principles which inform them and to renew our deeply held experience of them as organic and without self-contradiction. We can explore how each action becomes natural and self-fulfilled, and then we can repeat them regularly as an exercise, practice them, and grow into them with awareness until their new dimensions are quite familiar. These simplified experiences of movement can then be applied to the practicalities of the day's activity: playing the guitar, driving the car, digging in the garden.

The ideal can make itself known through both imagination and understanding: we form pictures, we think and compare, we make working hypotheses about which attitudes and responses are best for us and how we function most happily in sitting and moving. The ideal also reveals itself through reawakened experience. Most of us have at some time in our individual history expressed a buoyant and expansive living. Family albums contain photographs of us sitting in a playpen or highchair with a joyful upright balance to which we are giving no thought or effort. And there may have been later experiences where the integration of intention and physical doing has established a memorable harmony. Reconnecting with these moments of personal history can provide a potent touchstone for present change.

If we have made a commitment to a particular direction of change, there will most likely be a period, no matter with what determination and good faith the resolve has been made, when the old behavior will continue to assert itself, when we simply forget, some or most of the time. Or we remember, but still hang onto the old behavior, entirely or in part. With the deepest and most valued kinds of transformation this period can last many years, even a lifetime. Meeting golden moments of percipience with disappointment that we are still far from the ideal will make the occasion an unpleasant one and thereby reinforce forgetting.

Let's go back to Charlie for an example. Assume that he has come to a realization of the choice he made in the fifth grade when he identified with his ineptness. He sees now that his clumsiness in comparison with others was a stage of his development and that by freezing himself into an identification with it he has kept part of himself at that stage for 40 years. He sees that even now he can choose differently. His present posture expresses attitudes that perpetuate an undertow of disappointment, but he has gained an understanding of, and a feeling for, another postural pattern that will express him more positively and fully.

Charlie goes on about his life as a chemistry professor engrossed in writing a textbook. His body as he sits and writes has habitually fallen into compression, so that breathing and other organic functions are at a disadvantage and muscular tension around the neck and head creates eye-strain and headaches. These responses unnecessarily reinforce the idea that writing is difficult work. Charlie has written this way for many years. When he sits down to his task he mostly forgets his newfound knowledge and works as he always has. His focus of interest is after all chemistry.

But now and then he remembers. Perhaps his back hurts, or his eyes are blurring, or he senses that he could be breathing more easily or working with more humor and perspective. This is his golden moment, when he is doing the activity (writing) and at the same time is aware of it as a process. He is in Galileo's state of "suspicious inquiry," a state which is particularly delicate when he himself is the recipient of his attention. Charlie has every temptation, the training of those 40 years, to indulge in disgust at what he perceives, and if he chooses this path his golden moment evaporates—unless he is able to find a point of observation for witnessing the disgust itself, to see it too with the "detached eye" that renders it strange even while it is going on and that thereby breaks into his identification with it.

From his newly learned perspective Charlie sees his compression in contrast with an ideal. One choice is to shape up, particularly if his flash of awareness is accompanied by a negative reaction: he may snap himself into a more upright position—what we have called an imitation of the ideal—and abandon his old behavior so quickly that perception is minimal. But perceptivity is what he particularly needs in order to break the compulsiveness of the habit: its lack has allowed habit to form and become ingrained. And so Charlie does not shape up but stays just as he is and gives his golden moment its chance to play. He continues writing, continues being involved with his writing, continues in his compressed posture. With part of his consciousness he also takes all this in with the attitude of disinterested interest that his scientific training has taught him.

He is now in a state of sensory discernment where a shift toward the ideal can be full of insight, where he will be testing the ideal and not simply conforming to it—imitating it—and where his experience of it will shed additional light on his old habit. ("Ah, when I roll my pelvis forward like this, my chest opens and my head lifts. Now I'm breathing more easily, and my intellectual field of vision seems to be opening up. So is my ocular field of vision. There's a crick in my back that will be annoying pretty soon; let's see, if I sit more toward the front edge of the chair. . . .") All this flashes through him in seconds before his focus shifts again to his work.

Nurturing the golden moment: it presupposes a capacity to do at least two things at once, even to hold more than a single attitude toward an action. Artists and athletes perfect this capacity in themselves, and anyone draws on it who consciously develops a skill. Olympic divers give concentrated attention to their own movement while at the same time giving themselves fully to the action their movement accomplishes. They shift back and forth easily, even in the midst of a competition, between times when self-study is paramount (when they stand for seconds at the end of the diving board, feeling for balance under the moment's precise conditions of temperature, wind, mood) and times when pure action is foremost and conscious attention gives way to the play of reflex (when they have launched into a twist or a roll).

Charlie, like the diver, has come to realize that giving attention to the dynamic architecture of his own nerve/ muscle/bone system will enhance his performance. He too now allows the developing awareness of his own movement to serve his grand passion. He does not withdraw his attention from his work; while he writes, his perception of movement bubbles along in the current of his writing energy: how he is sitting, how he moves his arm to write or to sharpen a pencil. Sometimes his feeling for his movement is below the surface of consciousness, sometimes above. He may notice compression, he may gently alter it without interrupting his line of chemical thought. Now and again he may turn his full focus onto his movement. As he allows his "old" self to co-exist with what is developing, he gets better and better acquainted with himself.

Irony

A sense of humor is useful in nurturing the golden moment. When Charlie is smiling at himself he is not trivializing but is holding steady the double consciousness needed for witnessing his behavior while behaving. He is using irony, an intellectual device for uncovering and embodying complex truth. Paradox seems to emerge inevitably in considering questions of ultimate significance, even in physics. Are atoms particles or waves? And paradox cannot be held in the mind without irony. Paul's injunction to "work out your own salvation with fear and trembling, for it is the spirit of God which worketh in you" (*Philippians* 2:12–13), speaks ironically with a figure of speech that does justice to his experience and his thought about it. Paul's "fear and trembling" is, ironically speaking, Charlie's smile of self-recognition: the two seem to be opposites but they share a deep identity. Both are ways of being "at one" with the very thing separated out for attention.

Movement education, like any self-transformative project, is a bootstrap operation: you are working from a complex of present attitudes, ideas, motives, and values of which "debauched kinesthesia" is only one portion. Espousing an ideal different from present behavior provides part of the leverage necessary to grow, but it is not sufficient. Some negotiation which bridges between ideal and actual is needed, be it irony, a sense of humor, witnessing, scientific detachment, nonattachment, love, or generosity.

Principles of Transformation

As maple sap can be boiled down to its essential sweetness, some principles of self-determination can be summarized:

An ideal is not a model to be imitated but a hypothesis, a perspective from which to focus awareness on behavior and on the values behind behavior.

Staying with a problematic behavior in order to become fully aware of it, then changing it in order to observe the contrast, gives percipience a chance to do its work.

The guiding ideal functions most usefully when it is incorporated not only as image or idea but as action.

This possibility bears exploration: that a friendlier relation to the world is a natural birthright.

Moments of percipience are nurtured by being enjoyed. Patience with old behavior is more useful in a process of change than nagging.

Or if a negative reaction to old behavior surfaces (as part of the old behavior), a perspective for witnessing that reaction with detachment can be found.

A sense of humor helps sustain the perception of present behavior in the light of the guiding ideal.

Chapter 8

Generous Movement

There is in all visible things an invisible fecundity, a
dimmed light, a meek namelessness, a hidden wholeness. This mysterious unity and integrity is wisdom, the
mother of us all, "natura naturans." There is in all things
an inexhaustible sweetness and purity, a silence that is a
fountain of action and of joy. It rises up in wordless
gentleness, and flows out to me from the unseen roots of
all created being.

Thomas Merton, *A Hidden Wholeness* 1979, v

Generosity is an accurate single focus of meaning for the ideal
of human nature that we are exploring in this book. It is a
member of a rich family of words which are descended from
an ancient Indo-European root, *gen-, gon-,* or *gn-,* meaning
"give birth to." This root evolved through the Germanic languages into a spectrum of English meanings around *kin* (of
common birth) and includes the adjective *kind* (and its deriva-
tives, *kindness, kindly*). English also inherited a Greek and
Latin family of meanings descended from the same Indo-

European ancestor. *Generous* is a member of this clan. Other words from this Southern branch include *genius* (guardian spirit, prevalent disposition or spirit, innate capacity), *general* (pertaining to the whole), *genial* (nuptial, conducive to growth, cheerful, cheering, enlivening), *genesis* (creation), *genital*, and *benign*. *Nature* and *natural* (from Latin *nasci*, "be born") trace back to the same root. *Generous*, like *gentle*, once meant "nobly born" but came to describe more broadly the qualities attributed to those who are noble: that they are magnanimous, free in giving, ample.

Indo-European

gen-, gon-, gn-

Germanic

Greek and Latin

kin

kind, kindness, kindly

generous

genius

general

genial

genesis, generate

genital

benign

nature, natural

Generosity as Creative

Looking through the family of *gen-* words in order to illuminate what we mean by generosity as the heart of the human form or ideal, we might begin with *genesis* and *generate*, which descend directly from the ancient word in their reference to birth. A generous person lives from a core of creativity and growth. Meister Eckhart spoke of human life as a generative process in which the inmost core of the soul gives birth to God as the Son or Word. This process goes on at a level deeper than perception, idea, or feeling. "In that core is the central silence, the pure peace, and abode of the heavenly birth, the place for this event: this utterance of God's word" (Eckhart [14th century] 1941, 97). As we reach for an intuitive sense of ourselves, we may recognize something familiar in his paradox: that at our deepest we are at rest, peaceful, "at home"—and at the same time we are creative, an action or process, an "utterance." Thomas Merton articulates the same paradox in speaking of "a silence that is a fountain of action and of joy," though he is speaking not so much of individuality as of the totality of the world we live in—which of course includes ourselves. Eckhart and Merton are not spinning conundrums but are verbalizing their deepest realizations; in putting the word *generosity* at the center of our definition of humanness (including human movement) we too are dancing around the insight that humans are most themselves in this flowing world not in gathering or in "establishing" themselves but in sharing the process of creation.

For Rilke the role of humans is to transform the world by appreciating and artistically rendering the things in it. In doing so we make something spiritual of them and of ourselves.

> Are we perhaps *here* in order to say: house,
> bridge, well, gate, pitcher, fruit tree, window,—
> at most: column, tower. . . . but to *say*, understand it,
> oh to say as even the things never
> so fervently imagined themselves to be. (Rilke, *The Ninth Duino Elegy* [1923] 1989)

Transformation is for Rilke simultaneously a rendering of the forms of the world and a manifestation of our own form— these are in fact a single process of "giving birth."

A particular view of health is implied by the suggestion

that a human being is essentially, by definition, creative: that health is the process of growth and development. It unfolds continually. Just as species continue evolving in response to their internal and external environment, so on a faster scale does the individual. Childhood is only the most obvious phase of our growing, and when growth stops we are not "grown up" but ill. This is easiest to perceive when the symptoms are psychological: we are accustomed to thinking of neurosis as a problem of arrested development.

The word *genius*, which in Latin referred to the essential quality of an individual or, personalizing that essence, to a guardian spirit, bears witness to an ancient understanding that there is a generative kernel of being from which arises all the phenomenal complexity of the person, and which, if respected, will guide and protect. A genius like Einstein or Mozart is—so the word implies—a person who acts from the core of capability without self-obstruction. This is not to say that all geniuses are generous or that all generous people are geniuses but that both are true to themselves in a way that allows their actions to flow easily.

General means "pertaining to the whole." (Generals are people who run whole armies.) Generous people act totally; they don't withhold; they don't contradict their own actions. And at the same time they are in harmonious, "porous," responsive relationship to their whole environment. They stalk it: it attracts their caring attention and they are capable of seeing it for what it is, not for what they need to make of it.

Generosity as Natural

The word *nature* (from the Latin *nasci*, "be born," which in turn descends from the older *gen-* family) was once almost identical in meaning with *genius*: it referred to the essential quality of a person or a thing or of the totality of things: Mother Nature or "natura naturans." The word *natural* has come to refer often to the authenticity of the relationship between this essential or generative center and the "material" that embodies it. From this perspective a living tree is more natural than a telephone pole in that it more clearly expresses the essential form or generative power. A balanced body that releases its weight into movement is more natural than a chronically contracted one.

Generosity, being innate, is the most authentic expression of the individual, though it may lend itself to what Chögyam Trungpa (1973) calls spiritual materialism, an inversion of the hierarchy of values so that what is good is put to the task of demonstrating one's personal worth and becomes therefore merely an imitation of goodness. In itself generosity is innocent and neither cynical nor sentimental, both of which are self-interested states of consciousness.

To say that generosity is natural seems to fly in the face of a current of thought adapted from Darwin's theory of evolution. Darwinism holds that we humans, like all other living things, have evolved our present structure simply by surviving—by adapting to the demands of the world in which we live, by being "fit," that is, by fitting the environment. Darwinism translated from biology to social theory often assumes that the fittest humans are the most ruthless and selfish—those who are able to take from others.

This idea meshes nicely with the widely practiced ethical code of dog eat dog (a code which dogs do not practice), which is taught so pervasively that we often take it to be "natural." But biology does not support the notion that selfishness has promoted the survival of the human race, or that it bears any promise for the future. On the contrary, the practical experience of the last generation or two points strongly in the opposite direction, to the conclusion that the pursuit of individual interest, or the acquisitive interest of limited groups, is rapidly destroying us. We are ourselves one of the endangered species, and the ungenerous quality of our consciousness is at the heart of the problem. When we add the ever-growing empirical evidence—discussed in a note at the end of this chapter—that selfishness, recoil, and rigid, unloving behavior are bad for individual health, we have some scientific indicators to support the teaching of the major religions that generosity is good for us because it is the way we are designed to behave.

Generosity as Appreciative

The word *genial* picks up on the good-natured side of generosity and suggests by association that it is conducive to growth. Generous people not only live from their core of creativity but witness the natural depth of humanity, aliveness, and generosity in others and thereby nurture it. Cheerfulness is one of the hallmarks of generosity. An incident from Max's movement learning is illustrative. He had just finished playing for the movement class the fervent proclamation which opens Brahms' *Intermezzo*, Op. 118, No. 1. It had sounded curiously reserved and shallow in tone—competent surely, but stiff. The muscular pattern that constrained the sound was the same that sometimes tightened the fingers of his right hand into spasm.

He not only was alert to the limitations his listeners had noticed but was unduly hard on himself as he described what he had heard and felt. He commented that not only the music's fervor but his own, and his pleasure in playing, had been withheld. A taste of dust and ashes was a characteristic feeling for him in recitals. He chuckled, and went on to confess in a changed tone of voice that his attention had wandered while he was playing and he had remembered a dream. First had come the words: "Max, you are shying away!" Then followed a visual image of a horse, in two guises: one was himself as a handsome thoroughbred in a horse show, shying away from the grandstand, pawing the dirt anxiously, misbehaving; and at the next moment himself as thoroughbred, galloping along Wyoming slopes, mane and tail flying, sure-footed and exhilarated.

The perfect moment had arrived for the class to watch a videotape of a brief and loving imitation by Sammy Davis, Jr. of the tapdancer Bill Bojangles Robinson. Sammy Davis explains that Bojangles "always used to smile as he danced. Like this." He begins to dance, and with the footwork comes a broad smile, as if teased into utter delight by his performance, a smile which lights his entire face and body with its expression. It is guileless, and it penetrates the viewer with a directness that removes the distance between dancer and onlooker. You are engulfed in his goodwill and give yourself over to participating in the sheer pleasure of the movement as you watch and hear the complex rhythmic patterns of footfall under the graceful candor and nonchalance of the whole body's participation.

Still musing over Sammy Davis's presentation, the group did not notice that Max had walked back to the piano. He sounded Brahms's opening octave so dramatically that they were stunned. He smiled, tentatively at first, and swung ahead into the *Intermezzo*. Then a huge smile swept over his face. At the first big cadence he turned the beam of that smile toward his listeners and, still looking at them, swung on into the second big wave of sound. It was a smile of immense appreciation.

The magnificent sound was full-bodied, abandoned and yet secure, communicating phrase by phrase in a most intimate vein. It was such an astonishing performance and an astonishing Max that the class was moved to silence for many moments afterward. The "Bojangles smile" it became for them, this unfettered giving forth in performance.

Later Max spoke of this experience. He had felt for the

first time the spirit of his own generosity as he played and had realized that performance was indeed a complicated instance of generosity: on the part of the composer who generated the musical thoughts, on the part of the performer who reached out to listen with care and to master the composer's manner of speaking so that movement could bring it once again to life, and on the part of the audience, each person of which offered a breadth of human experience as resonator for composer and performer.

He realized that he had been operating from a point of view that recitals were an occasion to demonstrate a grasp of the difficult piano repertory and a mastery of what he assumed to be an inherently nerve-wracking situation. The audience was there to judge his success and failure—hopefully to admire him—and found this power to judge entertaining. And the composer had given him a series of hurdles, some scarcely superable, by which to "show his stuff."

His approach to practicing had fed into this view. Rehearsal was a time to get the notes down, get control over a passage, invent impressive interpretations that would give distinction to his playing. As he learned in the movement class to sit forward on the bench and lean toward the keys with more support from his legs and pelvis and with more spinal fluidity, he sensed a shift toward a happier and more giving style of musicianship, and now the idea of generosity, experienced so potently in his movement while playing, gave him a focused sense of direction.

He was optimistic that the attitudinal shift would alter his approach to practicing—that he would listen more carefully to the composer, would become more patiently and playfully exploratory, and would prepare himself for the role of sharing his appreciation rather than demonstrating his skill.

We intend that the word *generosity*, which stands at the center of our ideal of human behavior—and specifically of movement behavior—carry this whole complex of related meanings: generous behavior is creative and transformative; it is innate, natural, and authentic; it is sensitive, responsive, realistic; and it is joyful.

There is another aspect of generosity that makes it particularly appropriate as the keynote of movement transformation: that one is well served by turning generosity on oneself. If we hold an ideal of perfection, what a comfort it is to have that very perfection include tolerance, understanding, and affection for who we are right now in all our imperfections, and to know that taking a smiling attitude toward our problems is part of their solution. Generosity can make life downright enjoyable.

To be generous is, after all, to be loving not toward some notion I have of Lucy or of myself as she or I ought to be, but of the actual, characterized person who is here right now—and of the world in which we find ourselves. Generosity is allowing ourselves to be happy with actuality, with all its quirks and strange turns—even, somehow, with those things that hurt, disappoint, and anger us.

When Rilke speaks of transforming things, he does not mean changing them, but penetrating them with appreciation, which transforms not only them but us. We become more and more perfectly the creature who appreciates creation, who gives birth to it and therefore to ourselves. And we are ourselves one of the "things" that we transform—the richest and most fascinating of all, and the one we may come to know and love best. The ideal of generosity does not say, "I am what you should become," but "I am who you are. Please search me out and appreciate me."

Note

Selfishness, recoil, and rigidity have been discussed by Drs. Meyer Friedman and Ray Rosenman in their widely read book *Type A Behavior and Your Heart* (1974) as characteristic of persons who contract heart disease. For instance, one aspect of Type A behavior is an obsessive interest in sheer numerical acquisition, whether of dollars, athletic pennants, published articles, or monthly sales. Acquisition does not seem to satisfy the appetite for gain, nor does it fill the void of insecurity— of not being or having enough—around which such an obsession has wrapped itself. Another Type A trait is a "free-floating hostility" which tends to burst out uncontrollably and without justification, an aggressive version of recoil.

To be driven by a sense of time's urgency is a characteristic which may gradually rigidify responses to life's challenges and lead to compulsive and repetitious behavior: a precise schedule and sequence of gestures for showering, dressing, eating breakfast, and leaving for work; reading the same lecture notes year after year; using in a present business crisis the solution which worked last time. Larry Dossey's *Space, Time and Medicine* (1982) is a study of the relation of time perception to health.

The literature on stress as a psychophysical factor of heart disease, cancer, arthritis, asthma, and other ailments is expanding rapidly. Some authors approach the subject by encouraging readers to identify unhealthfully stressful situations and reactions, and then reprogram their lives to avoid them and to learn techniques of relaxation. See, for example, John W. Farquhar's *The American Way of Life Need Not Be Hazardous to Your Health* (1978). Others suggest that a shift of values is needed to cope with stress by dissolving it or rendering it ineffectual.

Hans Selye, in *Stress without Distress* (1974, 133–34), says that "to avoid the stress of conflict, frustration, and hate, to achieve peace and happiness, we should devote more attention to a better understanding of the natural basis of motivation and behavior. No one will be disappointed if, in daily life, he learns to follow the guiding light of 'Earn thy neighbor's love.' "

For Selye, generosity is a means for manipulating the environment in order to make life more livable; in our understanding it is the most fundamental expression of ourselves, even though it may take us a lifetime of learning, or rather of unlearning, to find the genuine article; if generosity reduces stress by earning rewards, that is incidental to the fact that it is our most authentic form of self-expression. See also Selye's *The Stress of Life* (1956) the classic work by the man who persuasively educated both medical professionals and laymen on the distinction between healthy and unhealthy stress and the significance of the latter as an identifiable physical syndrome present in all disease.

For a discussion of healthful stress, see S. G. Pickering, *Exercises for the Autonomic Nervous System* (1981). Norman Cousins, in *Anatomy of an Illness* (1981) and *The Healing Heart* (1983) discusses the significance of good-naturedness and mirth in the healing of a disease syndrome. Both he and the Simontons (in *Getting Well Again* 1978, which deals with cancer) describe steps which may be taken to assume responsibility for one's disease and to cope with it by positive imagery and alert sensibility.

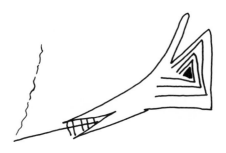

Core support mobilizes the pelvic girdle so that its strength is delivered to one's actions. The two men leaning over to lift bales of hay are straining their backs, shoulders, and arms because their legs are not being utilized to advantage. The baby, the racquetball player, and the two men cinching the mule are all demonstrating effective core support.

If the upper body leans a little in front of the vertical, the weight is placed over the arches. Then spaciousness up the front of the pelvis and along the lumbar spine—in the big hip flexors—makes a solid connection between legs and trunk.

Chapter 9

Core Support
Mobilizing Strength

Again, the kingdom of heaven is like unto a merchant-
man, seeking goodly pearls: Who, when he had found
one pearl of great price, went and sold all that he had,
and bought it.
   Matthew 13: 45–46

Mobilizing Pelvic Girdle Strength

The 24 university students who had shown up for the first
movement awareness class of the semester were diverse:
some athletes, musicians, and dancers who wanted to improve specific skills or deal with problems of recurrent pain,
and others who were looking for more graceful and peaceful
ways to live. Thomas's friend Nicki, who took a professional
interest in his work, was visiting for the afternoon.

Three or four introductory processes to invite playful and comfortable movement had relieved much of the nervousness that was at first hovering in the room, and Thomas now asked them to move in slow continuous motion, imagining that their hands and feet were molding a large sculpture in front of and around them. Their feet were to remain planted. The room hushed as a quiet piece of music for bamboo flute began. Here and there an edgy giggling would break out, ripple through the people nearby and subside.

Gradually Thomas's gaze was attracted by five individuals scattered about the room. The movement palette of each was unmistakably personal, with little similarity between them in range, tempo or shape; and yet these five had something in common. He passed his gaze back over all the others. What was it about the way most were moving? They stood fixed: legs spread, knees locked, the lower half of the body braced. Their movements, localized mainly in arms and shoulders, did not play through. And the attention of these students seemed either distracted by interior thoughts or self-consciously given to the invention of one maneuver and then another.

Looking back at the five, he saw that their feet were planted and yet were supple with movement that mediated between the solidity of earth and the mobility above. Knee and hip joints were flexibly adapting to the movements which, though most animated in the upper torso, neck and arms, were continuously reflected in the lower part of the body. Matching this fuller physical participation, they appeared to have a more inclusive awareness of others in the room; *compassionate* was the word that came to Thomas's mind.

As Thomas and Nicki sat in the quiet of her patio after class, Thomas used the term *core support* to describe the quality of movement he had observed. "You know, I usually teach this principle far into the semester, after many experiences of balance and weight have established a context for it. But to-day—the first class of the semester—was a reminder that core support is innate. Those five who are already functioning with core support, probably without ever giving it a deliberate thought, can develop and perfect it as the principle becomes clear; the others can rediscover what their bodies have forgotten."

"Exactly what do you mean by core support?" As a practitioner of structural integration, Nicki worked from the same principles as Thomas but with a different technique. Structural integration, designed by Nicki's teacher Ida Rolf, is a deep systematic manipulation which stretches the body's connective tissue. Dr. Rolf discovered that applying appropriate pressure to connective tissue can change the habitual tension level of muscles, sometimes quickly and dramatically. The work systematically alters the pattern of muscular tensions that determines how the body balances and moves in gravity. Nicki and Thomas frequently referred clients or students to one another and enjoyed the opportunity to discuss ideas since their goal was similar but their methods quite different. Their discussions were animated by the contrast of their backgrounds—Nicki's in engineering and Thomas's in music.

Thomas smiled at her question and began with a high-toned metaphor sure to provoke her. "Core support is the upthrust of the earth's energy through the body. When we rest into it we tap our source of vitality."

Nicki took up the challenge. "What we rest into is the skeleton. Core support, as you call it, integrates movement so that the pelvic girdle participates fully with the shoulder girdle. Each part contributes according to its capacity."

"Not bad," said Thomas. "So we agree that core support has to do with vertical polarity, the way top and bottom function together, whether we're talking about energy or structure."

Nicki continued. "Those who know a little about our work say that we get people to stand up straight. They recognize that the work is about balance. The idea of core support allows us to talk about balance in action. Why do people who are mobilizing their vitality assume a crouching stance? You see it in every baseball game, whether the focus is on quickness, with the shortstop watching the batter, or on power, with the batter waiting for the pitch, or on accuracy, with the pitcher winding up. The crouch is a natural way to gather energy. Stalking cats crouch."

Nicki stood up suddenly and assumed the slight-squatting stance of the martial artist. "I'm ready to kick, strike, jump or run in any direction." Growling aggressively, she leaped around the patio, each time landing with both feet at once and dropping into a slight-squatting position. "Your five students were using their pelvic girdles."

Thomas, laughing, said she reminded him of hopping robots he had lately seen on television. "They looked like powered pogo sticks."

"That's a pretty good image, actually," said Nicki, demonstrating as she went on. "The essence of crouching is to flex the knees and hips. This lengthens the strongest muscles in the body and sets them up for a contraction which pushes the feet against the ground. Just like the spring in a pogo stick."

Thomas imitated a few of Nicki's two-footed leaps to confirm in his own joints and muscles what she was saying. In the meantime Nicki had found a towel in the corner and gone over to the kitchen window. "Look, when I wash the windows I swirl the cloth around and push. If I stand straight-legged, not much of the push can come from my legs, so I have to contract my shoulders and do most of the work with my arms.

"But the obvious structural difference between top and bottom suggests that there can be a more effective distribution of effort. The pelvic girdle is the power train. The shoulder girdle, lighter and more differentiated, is the steering mechanism, designed for control. Pushing the cloth comes best from the pelvic girdle, swirling the cloth comes best from the shoulder girdle. If I use my legs for power, my shoulders and arms can relax and better guide that power into the task."

"If it's good for shortstops and window washers, why not everybody?" asked Thomas as they sat down again. "Do you recommend that people crouch when they stand and walk?"

"No," said Nicki, "someone walking the dog doesn't require the power of someone beginning a sprint. They can mobilize pelvic and leg muscles for an easy walk without any extra flexion, and it's more efficient to keep the body long, so that the center of gravity is higher and body weight can fall forward into movement. You find core support in walking not by exaggerated knee flexion but by allowing body weight to center across the arches rather than into the heels. The arch is like a shock absorber or a spring—it provides a lift, part of the upthrust you were talking about. If the upper body leans a little in front of the vertical, the weight is placed over the arches. Then spaciousness up the front of the pelvis and along the lumbar spine—in the big hip flexors—makes a solid connection between legs and trunk. It lets the power flow up into the shoulder girdle."

"The issues are the same for sitting, aren't they?" said Thomas. "The tilt of the pelvis is usually the crucial factor in teaching people better support. If they sit on the tailbone, tipping the pelvis back, the hip flexors are thrown out of commission. The weight of the body settles against the chair in a sluggish clump. Movements of the upper body, lacking foundation, are restricted and overstrained. The supportive power of the legs and feet is cut off. But if a person sitting to do something—typing, say, or sewing or eating—poises upper body weight on top of their sitting bones and, by swaying the whole trunk forward slightly, distributes their weight between sitting bones on the chair and their feet on the floor, then their legs can actively participate. Sitting on the front edge of a chair with a solid seat will maximize support and mobility." Thomas drew a couple of sketches.

"Looking at your sketches," said Nicki, "I can certainly see that the leaning person has core support, and can imagine that the reaching motions—forward to insert paper in the typewriter or sideways for a dictionary—will originate in both ankle and hip joints and engage the entire body. It strikes me how much this sitting resembles the standing crouch; only now, rather than perching over two feet, the person perches on four points: two sitting bones and two feet.

Span

"But let me take a different tack with core support. I usually observe at closer range than you do, with the client lying on a table. One of my hard-earned skills in practicing structural integration is to be able to watch the outward contours of the skin and recognize changes in connective tissue, sometimes two or three inches deeper. When fascia releases, the muscle reorganizes its shape and you can see core support in a specific sense.

"Ida Rolf called this tissue-quality span. Spanned flesh is spacious, alert, potent with mobility even when still. For instance, when I'm working at the bottom of the rib cage I watch for span between the lower ribs and the pelvis. A suppleness comes into breathing movement, an interweaving from each moving part to the next. When the client stands, the rib cage seems to float buoyantly above the pelvis."

"If core support is a matter of vertical polarity," said Thomas, "what does span have to do with it?"

"Span is core support in fine detail—the way flesh itself, perhaps even at the cellular level, deals with gravity when it is part of a balanced structure. Tensegrity is suggestive of human structure, but mechanical models made with sticks and wires distinguish too sharply between soft and hard, tension and compression, muscle and bone. I know I said that the skeleton forms our support, but spanned soft tissue gives the impression of being itself supportive, as if within it were tiny tensegrity structures that become light, spacious, elastic—and supportive—when they are properly adjusted to gravity. Dr. Rolf, who was originally a biochemist, saw span as a particular chemistry of the tissue."

Vertical Polarity

"You see," said Thomas, "we're getting back to my opening statement that core support is a flow of energy. Have you ever taken any interest in chakra balancing?" Nicki confessed it had seemed no more than hocus-pocus for her; she had never been sufficiently intrigued to explore it. "It works with energy centers along the core of the body," continued Thomas, "to quiet some centers and intensify others, depending on need. The root chakra, at the base of the spine, is the center of grounding energy and power; the heart chakra, of loving energy; the brow chakra, of wisdom. It's not really as mysterious as it sounds." He asked her to focus attention for a few moments on each of the three locations he had mentioned, the root, the heart and the brow, one at a time, and to become conscious of its distinctive feeling tone.

"Each place certainly feels different from the others," Nicki said quietly after two or three minutes. "They're ordinary feelings, and probably have always been there without my noticing them. It's hard to describe. Something like a hum or a buzz, the sense of being alive in that particular place. The pelvis resonates with a slower vibration, like the notes at the lower end of the musical scale. The head vibration is higher and lighter—more playful, at least right at the moment."

"That's another indication of vertical polarity," Thomas pointed out. "Don't your vibrational perceptions match your understanding of the different functions of the pelvic and shoulder girdles, one more ponderous and strong, the other more refined and skillful? The goal of finding physical balance is similar to the goal of chakra balancing, to bring the parts into harmonious relationship so that each plays its characteristic role, cooperating with the others and now and again predominating when appropriate, but not persistently or at the expense of the others."

Nicki nodded thoughtfully. "Wilhelm Reich was working with a similar idea from a psychological perspective. Armoring separates head energy from pelvic energy and keeps them from streaming together. But I don't think Reich gave much attention to gravity. When armoring pulls body weight off its axis, gravity creates a mechanical need for rigidity. To regain consistent streaming—the flow of vitality—requires that a person be living in physical balance."

"It seems useful for teaching purposes," replied Thomas, "to have both mechanical and energy-flow models. What we understand as skeletal support to which we can give our-selves with a sense of security, may be felt more clearly as a current of strength. Support has a depth dimension. Medita-tion teachers are usually insistent about the physical attitude of the body. It's funny that while core support may be an attribute of movement in a person who is getting things done, whose body is being the efficient instrument of practi-cal intention, it's also the optimum style for meditation—for the person who in terms of gross physical action is doing nothing at all."

Nicki went into the house and returned thumbing through Suzuki Roshi's *Zen Mind Beginner's Mind* to find this passage:

> You should be sitting straight up as if you were support-ing the sky with your head. . . . These forms are not a means of obtaining the right state of mind. To take this posture itself is the purpose of our practice. When you have this posture, you have the right state of mind, so there is no need to try to attain some special state. (1970, 26)

"But some of us," said Nicki as she finished reading, "need an arena for learning that isn't just sitting still. Think-ing of vertical polarity as a function of bones, muscles and joints gives us an ideal we can refer to when we're digging in the garden or playing the oboe."

Core Support as an Expression of Attitude and Values

Thomas thought of Janie. "I've been working with one of my private clients on vacuum cleaning. She'd take a wide stance, lock her knees and push forward and back from this position, mostly with her arms. The strain to her shoulders and neck would move up and settle in as a headache. Now she's learning to step forward as she pushes. This gives her back leg the position it needs to power the push; her forward leg catches her body weight and then powers the pulling back of the vacuum cleaner. And so the strain in her upper body is relieved. In fact, she finds she can use vacuum cleaning as a loosening exercise to release tension." Thomas drew more sketches.

"She's also been realizing that lack of core support has been an expression of martyrdom—that vacuuming is *her* task. Learning to give herself to it and find what pleasure there can be in it involves more than mastering a skill; she has to unravel the assumption that she would betray herself if she enjoyed this menial chore.

"You demonstrated vertical imbalance in energy expenditure when you washed the window without core support: arms tight, shoulders elevated, chest slumped, face strained, pelvis and legs relatively uninvolved. But someone who washes windows or vacuums this way will generally show the same energy configuration when they're inactive. That's what Reich was driving at: there is a psychological state, an attitude, prior to any particular activity. Not always martyrdom, of course; if you had to put a single psychological tag on it, I suppose 'anxiety' would be the most broadly applicable."

"I liked what you told your class today," said Nicki. "That finding core support in oneself is a direct, simple way to transform attitudes. Old value structures won't just go up in smoke, but working with their bodily expression gives a person the chance to shift what is actual in their life, what is embedded in acts."

As Thomas walked home, letting a background sense of core support play through his movements, quieting and strengthening him, he thought of something else he had said to his students earlier in the afternoon: that in the realm of movement, core support is the one pearl of great price.

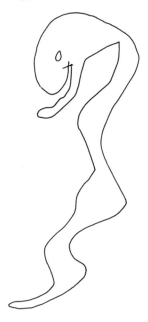

Chapter 10

Reverberation
Letting Action Through

I do not know which to prefer,
The beauty of inflections
Or the beauty of innuendoes,
The blackbird whistling
Or just after.
> Wallace Stevens,
> *Thirteen Ways of Looking*
> *at a Blackbird*, 1957, 93

Reverberation as the Shimmer of Action

Reverberation is the play of aliveness, the shimmer of action through the body. As ripples circle out from a pebble dropped in a pond, vibratory response is prompted when we move.

But these waves of internal response are easily choked by residual tension, or withheld by the habit of darting from one not-quite-completed task to the next, leaving a trail of the almost-finished. They are muffled by distraction and half-heartedness or by the image many hold of themselves as lumpish, "too, too solid flesh," not tremulously alive.

Witnessing reverberation in the unselfconscious movement of animals and plants can be suggestive as we begin to unlock a similar abandon and let motions take their effect through us. For this reason, Thomas often showed his students a film about animals moving (*Nova*, "Animal Olympians," 1980). It was easy to see the meandering wriggles of reverberation in the ample flesh of an Arctic seal as it belly-flopped along the ice or propelled itself by sideways tail-swishes. And in the ostrich taking broad strides across an African plain, the echoes of each footfall could be observed in the quivering of tail-, side-, and underfeathers, in the jiggling flesh of the thighs, and in the slower back-and-forth oscillations of the long neck. Even tongues gave visible response, flapping in the slightly open mouths of antelope as they ran through the brush. The students, having seen their reverberative image in these other creatures, could feel it more easily within themselves and consciously incorporate it as an underlay of their movement.

A quick way to sense the significance of reverberation is deliberately not to allow it. Jump off the floor, or imagine jumping. Brace yourself as you land. Tighten everything. Notice the uncomfortable jolt.

Then dampen reverberation by limpness: jump and land, letting yourself give way to the impact, reserving only enough tonus not to crumple to the floor. On landing you find yourself in a dropped position, knees and ankles bent, arms and head hung forward. The jolt of the braced-against landing has been replaced by a diffused heaviness and discomfort in your legs as they strain to hold you up.

For contrast, deliberately allow reverberation. Jump, and as you land let yourself rebound with the impact, your body righting itself in vibratory movements which true you around the vertical axis. The whole action is buoyant. Unless you are as lax as Sambo's tiger reduced to melted butter or as stiff as the Tin Woodman of Oz, you inevitably reverberate as you jump and land, and as you otherwise move about.

If you are on a wooden floor you can hear the difference between the three modes of jumping. With a braced landing the sound of the impact is clipped; with a flopped landing, muffled. When the landing is reverberant, the sound itself has buoyancy; it is articulate without being clipped and the overtones play freely, giving depth and fullness. The quality of sound reflects the quality of touch upon landing. Tactile and auditory information arising from contact with the floor measures internal adaptations to the action of jumping and landing.

You can observe in a mirror the reverberative movements of breathing. If you watch your lower rib cage expand as you inhale, any point will seem to be a center from which everything else moves away. The more deeply reverberative the movement, the smaller are the units that play in relation to one another. Pretend to be frightened or angry, or slouch so that added weight presses down on the area you are watching, and the smaller increments of movement disappear. Come into better balance and allow weight to be suspended, and a more refined flow of reverberative action and reaction resumes. It was this quality of interconnection in the tissue that Nicki watched for in her clients' breathing, as evidence that her structural integration work had released chronic tension and induced span in the tissue.

Throwing Weight

A jump lifts weight vertically, but for most of our daily activities we throw weight forth horizontally to extend ourselves into the semicircle before us. Innumerable times during the day we throw our weight off its central axis and then recover it, coming to transient repose around the vertical, like a tree being gusted in the wind. Planted at a temporary base, we yield ourselves forward to expressive impulse whether to speak, play an instrument, or throw a frisbee; finishing, we return to upright, oscillating into poise through vibratory movements which ramify everywhere in the body. In walking, reactive waves set up by each individual footfall blend into those of the next and form a continuous vibrating response visible not only in arm-swings but in bobs of the head and in the still smaller quaking of fleshy surfaces. Each of the countless actions of a day, be it ever so insignificant or outside the need for conscious notice, calls for an appropriate blend of stabilizing and yielding.

Reverberation arises when parts of the body are allowed to be elastic in their relations with one another. As a variation on the tensegrity model, you might picture the flesh to be a collection of tiny balloons filled with water and suspended by rubber bands from the skeletal framework and from one another, with enough play in the rubber bands that any movement sets up a liquid ripple of response. The balloons are organized hierarchically: they contain within them collections of smaller balloons that resonate together as a group, and the smaller ones contain groups of still smaller balloons, and so forth down to subcellular levels. There is a play of individual freedom at all levels of organization, the amount of play varying according to need since there is also an unimaginably complex control system that can alter the give in the rubber bands and in the skin of each of the balloons.

Paradoxically, movement becomes whole only when the parts are sufficiently free from one another that the weight of each can fall, swing through, and have its expression. When unity is enforced by unneeded tension, the parts obstruct one another and the swing-through of weight is encumbered. If the arm reaching out for the doorknob is locked at the shoulder joint, the expansive ripple of reverberation from torso out into arm is cut off; if a leg swinging forward in walking does not fall a little, opening the hip joint, if its weight is not allowed to assert itself, then reverberation will be crude and chunky and the adaptation of legs to trunk in balancing and controlling movement will be correspondingly less refined.

Integrated Spinal Movement

The fountainhead of reverberation is the balanced spine. Optimally, any action taking the body off its central axis calls for the spine to lengthen. The weight of the head is poised, ready to swing into action, and when it swings it gathers momentum, which is then energy available for whatever one is doing. Since the spine is flexible, the moving weight of the head will set up an expansive release along its length. The muscles that are woven around the spine can stabilize and at the same time release so that each intervertebral joint with its waterbedlike disk adapts to the movement, allowing momentum to gather and give force to actions. The dynamics would be similar if you impaled an orange on the upper end of a sturdy green willow stick, pulled the top of the shaft sideways, released it, and then let it oscillate. The spine has a similar capacity for that springiness. Watch the trunks of slender trees or blades of tall grass blown by the wind.

This gentle whipping action of the spine is not the norm in our culture. If you were to lean forward at this moment and pick an imaginary flower growing in the air in front of you about four feet away, and were to repeat this gesture a number of times so that you could focus your awareness on the movement of your head and neck, you might make the discovery that launched F. M. Alexander on his career as a movement teacher: that he pulled his head backward as his trunk swayed forward, shortening the nape of his neck. If the head is thus retracted, the spinal curves of neck and upper back do not lengthen into the movement of reaching but contract and then brace against the reach. Alexander began his explorations because he was losing his voice in dramatic performances. He was able, through careful observation, to link this vocal problem with his habit of head retraction; the muscles of his neck and throat participated in this shortening of the cervical spine, impeding breath and straining the process of speech.

When there is integrated functioning of the spine, the head, perched on top, is anchored by the pelvis. The head nods slightly, with muscular tonus, into a reach, and the entire spine, particularly of the neck, lengthens so that intervertebral joints open and each of the disks with its rocking articulation shares in the movement. As with the oscillating green willow stick with an orange on top, there are no sharp breaks in the supportive movement, but a single integrated flow of bending.

The release of the head into forward reaching depends on an interactive release of the back muscles. One of Ida Rolf's maxims—the title of a chapter in her book *Rolfing: The Integration of Human Structures*—is that "in a balanced body, when flexors flex, extensors extend" (1978, 65). When the muscles on the front of the trunk flex, or shorten, to bend it forward, the muscles on the posterior side extend, or lengthen; they release little by little, creating a matrix of support so that each of the spinal joints can exercise its appropriate capacity for movement. This toned expansion of the back is part of the control for reaching; both finesse and strength depend on its being precisely appropriate to the action. If extensors fail to release sufficiently, or instead contract during the swing forward (as they did in F. M. Alexander's neck), their pull will contradict the action undertaken.

Like a musical tone, whose purest and fullest resonance is liberated when the pitch is perfectly centered, the most truly shaped and deeply penetrating reverberation will result when the tissue is spanning—that is, when the body acts with commitment of weight and then counterbalances around a supportive and expansive core.

Reaching is by far the most common of our movements. We do it thousands of times each day: to eat, drive, open and close, push, pull, throw, give, and take. Most of these actions are routine, transitory, hardly noticed components of larger purposes. If each one adds a tiny element of tension, shortens the spine, and ties the knot a little tighter by steeling muscles against movement, the cumulative effect in fatigue, discomfort, wear and tear, and psychological strain may be enormous. On the other hand, if each one embodies integrated spinal movement, there is a release that lengthens the spine, gently kneading tissues, pumping fluids, and dispersing unproductive emotions. Ordinary activity becomes an ongoing source of refreshment.

To summarize and proceed: since the majority of our motions swing body weight off its central axis, it is important that they be integrative and nourishing. The instigating head-toss draws along a flexible and yielding spine, which in turn evokes a stretching of the body into the action. The toss of weight off center is anchored by the pelvic girdle; the anchor itself is planted, feet on the ground (and, if we are sitting, buttocks on the chair). The body then swings back toward center and oscillates until the waves of motion have completed themselves and full resting length has been restored.

Why do head retraction and spinal shortening, instinctive for startled or cringing reactions and usefully immobilizing there, so permeate motions undertaken when we are clearly not in danger? Are we so enmeshed in anxiety and fearfulness that they continually plague us? Are we each such enslaved imitators of the cultural norm that we cannot separate from it and sense inwardly what would be native as a style of moving forth into activity? Perhaps we have been taught immobility by a sedentary existence, with its postural customs of collapsing, of leaning heavily against furniture, of being enthralled by passive forms of entertainment. If we are sunken into an inert clump, we are not in a position to move easily, to swing our weight or let it fall from a mobile perch, but need to push ourselves forth. Furthermore, time-driven as many of us are, we are likely to begin even slow movements "off the bat": like a knee jerking to the tap of the doctor's hammer we suddenly are in motion, almost surprised, not fully having made the decision to move and not even entirely aware that we are moving. Our responses are indeed startled. And we shorten our spines to secure these arms and legs as they sally forth.

Reaching and Seeing

Reaching and reverberation are intertwined with seeing. The visual pattern characteristic of head retraction differs from that of integrated spinal movement, and the latter may feel awkward or even unsuitable until the eyes have made the necessary adaptation. When Dan reached for the welding torch, his habitual head retraction framed his visual field in a particular way: his eyes remained immobile, focus set on the welding torch, while his head drew back.

When he altered the motion of his head to nod forward with the reach, the plane of his face shifted downward so that it was necessary either for his eye muscles to actively roll his eyes upward, in order to keep the welding torch in central view, or else for him to keep sight of the torch with peripheral vision. Dan, trained by long habit to a tight visual focus, was uncomfortable at first and said that he couldn't see what he was doing. It was necessary for him to accustom himself consciously to this more mobile base for his eyes, and to use peripheral vision actively in order for old visual habits not to continue prompting him into head retraction.

The impulse to be looking constantly with central vision is part of a psychophysical syndrome which includes spinal fixation as another characteristic. Tunnel vision—the use of the macula, or central portion of the retina, to the relative exclusion of the surrounding area—is hard on eyes and diminishes their visual potential; it accentuates selective fixation upon objects one after another, missing the whole view and seeing objects as separate from their larger context. It accompanies and fortifies a tunneling habit of mind, a tendency to fasten onto particular issues or circumstances, to hold doggedly and sometimes with exaggerated emotionality to a point of view, and to be unable to contextualize or to find fresh responses.

Varieties of Reverberation

To look behind himself, Harry retracts his head and flips it around, chin jutted forward and up, while holding his trunk still; Max arches his back and fixes his spine, then turns his whole body as a chunk. To lift a box from the table and set it onto a high shelf, Janie compresses her spine, deepening all its curves, while her shoulder girdle lifts up the weight. Bending to the side to pick up a suitcase, Charlie retracts his head and crumples his lower vertebrae into an exaggerated curve.

Integrated spinal action unlocks and eases these turning, lifting, and bending movements. Throws of weight into action will resound along the entire spine. When one is looking over the shoulder, head weight can swing the neck into a rotation which then ripples down through the spine from atlas to anchoring sacrum; the body remains on its gravitational axis, turned by the upper spine, whose length is maintained throughout the turn by the fostering of spaces between the vertebrae. To lean slightly backwards and reach for a high shelf, or sideways for the suitcase, the throw of head weight echoes along the spine and lengthens it into a soft arc.

For any movement there is an ideal reverberation. Sometimes whipping movements—quick pushes from a necessarily girding structure—are called for. Imagine a quick head-turn to see the car which has just honked. Reverberation is first localized at the nape of the neck and then suffuses. Other movements may need to be slow and sustained—putting the needle down on a recording or tiptoeing through a room where a baby is asleep. Rather than free-swinging footfalls, the body organizes itself firmly and movement oozes out in a steady, controlled stream. There is almost no separation of time between each increment of the tiptoeing and its echoing reaction.

To experience reverberation in this sustained style of movement, Thomas's class often did a slow-motion improvisation which the group called "Source and Respondent." Accompanying a sustained and melodic piece of music, one person would begin to move. Perhaps the right arm went slowly outward. The partner, observing this arm to be the point of origin (source) of the movement, would watch for a response further away in the body and then lightly tap that place. The left side, for example, might bend gradually to counterbalance the right arm's outward gesture. The mover would let the tapped left side become the new source for the continuously flowing movement, and the observing partner would watch for the next location of obvious response and again tap. At first the slow motion would go in halting spurts whose reflections elsewhere in the body were faint. As the taps made clear to the mover that even the smallest movements create waves, the intervening flesh was increasingly pervaded by the shimmer of shifting and releasing weight.

No two movements are identical. Even in a repetitive action such as the strokes when brushing your hair, each has a slightly different pressure, length, and intermingling with the hair. The reverberant hue reflecting these differences can be seen by an observer and sensed from within.

Follow-through

Except where two actions abut or overlap, reverberation ends well beyond what we may be accustomed to consider completion. Marion, placing a coffee cup on the table, decides to be alert until the simple action—including all aspects of the effort summoned—has completely resolved into stillness. She puts the cup down. The activity of resolution in hand, arm, shoulder, and back after the cup safely contacts the table is complex; she is astonished that it could have gone unnoticed. For contrast she repeats the action, purposely re-creating how she ordinarily sets down the cup. Even before it has quite landed she notices that her attention has flicked elsewhere, and that a residue of muscular contraction has been left which becomes noticeable as she goes on to the next action—say, reaching her hand out to turn the page. She consciously releases the residue and thereby completes the reverberation of the cup-placing action even while in the midst of turning the page. Though delayed, the coming to rest of that previous effort gives her a perceptible sensation of relief.

This experiment might suggest that reverberation neces-sarily requires a long time to subside. But the time needed, the route through the body, and the qualities of release de-pend on an action's motivation, on the speed, size, and shape of its execution, and on whether and when it is allowed to penetrate the system. Reverberation can complete itself in the instantaneous wash-through of an abrupt gesture, or in a gradual dwindle over many seconds.

The resounding of an action affects not just its conclusion but its whole course. If the final downward flourish in the swing of a tennis serve has been cut short, the direction, speed, and distance of the ball's flight to the opponent's court will be adversely affected; if a pitcher does not allow head and trunk to complete the trajectory of their arc, the pitch itself will be limited in drive and spin. Athletes practice "fol-low-through," the deliberate full reverberation of the end of an action, knowing that their attention to this final phase will be repaid in the power and accuracy of the entire action.

Some actions complete themselves off balance: resolu-tion of an action is not equivalent to rest, if we define rest as being restored around the vertical. Sometimes movements must reverberate in the heat of gesture, often at the peak of their muscular effort. A golf putt near the hole may depend for its accuracy on coming to an abrupt stop, all aspects of the bent-forward stance steadied. A quick arm gesture outward to stop a bag of groceries from tipping off the table must breathe its reverberant sigh of relief within an apparently frozen ending.

Wind-up

Reverberation begins in the hazy realm preceding action, where thinking to do first gives way to intending and then doing. If I reach to the knob to turn it and open the door, reverberation will be determined by the specific reason for doing this, by the feelings that inform the reason and by my capacity to do the present deed without an obfuscating trail of door-opening habits which bar me from sensitivity to the very moment. "Present mirth hath present laughter." Think of the difference between opening the door cautiously at night to mysterious knocking and opening it in the afternoon to an expected delivery of roses.

For weight to be released into action so that its momentum can undulate resonantly through the body, it first has to be mustered by a gathering, a wind-up. It occurs as a swing, often small and scarcely perceptible, in the direction opposite to the movement about to be made. As Max practiced integrated use of his spine at the piano, he noticed that before he swayed forward to play a phrase, his trunk and head swung a little back; this collected weight was then tossed into the forward motion. Karen, a flutist, perceived a similar slight backward swing of her head and upper torso as she completed the inhalation readying her to sound the notes of the next phrase; she also noticed a slight forward throw of head weight—

anchored in the pelvis by a subtly expansive spine—as she began the exhalation to produce tone. She realized that she had developed a habit of stabilizing her spine against these innate, tiny motions, probably in the attempt to hold steady the desired embouchure as her lower lip rested lightly on the instrument. But the embouchure improved when its positioning was not so tightly enforced. Learning to release the suboccipital muscles, delicate fomentors and balancers of head-nods in the neck just beneath the base of the skull, helped her to increase inhalation and gave her more control over the flow of breath during exhalation. Her tone steadied and rounded.

She applied the same principle to speaking as she coached her high school band classes. Before commenting on a passage just muddled through by her players, she let her head nod a little back to complete the inhalation and then gently swung it forward onto her words. Without straining she could project to all in the group, and the slight delay granted by the wind-up helped her choose more measured remarks than the snappish criticisms that first sprang to mind.

Thomas had heard the ballet dancer Makarova speak in a televised interview of the "and" before a movement begins. This "and" became a cue for an experiment that his movement classes found valuable, to catch the feel of the wind-up and practice it in various contexts. First, they would take a commonplace activity, such as walking, and coach themselves by speaking aloud the imperative "Walk!" On the instant of command, they would begin the action. Then, in contrast, they ordered, *"And* walk!" Without any discussion as to what might happen differently, they discovered that on the *and*—said with a slightly exaggerated upbeat quality—there occurred, as if by reflex, a wind-up. The body mobilized around the resting axis and seemed to grow potent with in-tention, head and trunk swung back a bit; as the verb arrived, walking began on a lilt of momentum. When they tried again without the *and*, they noticed that upon the command "Walk!" the body compacted itself and jolted into motion. Reverberation was withheld right from the start of the action. The distinction was similar with other actions: turning, lifting an arm, sitting down. In each case, the upbeat, upswinging *and* served as an intaken breath whose outflow cast forth the movement.

Developing a Vocabulary of Reverberation

Whereas Dan's withholding of spinal expansion was most noticeable at the neck, in Max's case retraction was char-acteristic of the whole back, from pelvis to head. As he reached forward to strike the piano keys, his arched back was firmed in opposition to the downward thrust of arms and fingers.

In addition to healing the spasms of his hand, the release of this nonreverberant pattern resulted in richer and fuller tone. In mechanical terms, Max learned to free the holding at his hip joints so that the pelvis swayed his torso toward the keyboard; relaxing his back, he allowed the spine to lengthen; his head bobbed gently forward, contributing its weight to the impact of his fingers against the keys. The rotation of his forearm, which successively brought different fingers into action against the keys, benefited from this contribution of weight from his trunk and head: quick runs across the keyboard became more supple, and he noticed that it was easier to keep his wrist from tightening into a stressful sideways twist, out of alignment with his forearm. In broader terms, he allowed more of himself to swing into the making of tone. Every joint in his body contributed to the color and rhythm of the notes, so that the action resulting in sound was focused, singleminded, and intimate; the parts that had been holding back and contradicting were now joining in.

During the search for playing options that would be more resilient physically and musically, Max found that he needed to reconsider precepts about piano technique absorbed long ago, often thoughtlessly, that still shaped his understanding. He ordinarily spoke of finger action as "lifting," then "hitting," "striking," or "pressing into" the keys, and of arm action as "lifting," "thrusting," or "dropping." Now, he noticed that his fingers made arcing *swings* from the palmar joints and that these freely issuing swings had sufficient power to depress the piano keys. The use of these tiny weight-throws and their momentum kept the muscular tissue of the hand and finger maximally open so that it could span supportively when positioned upon the keyboard. He noticed that his forearm also made arced swinging motions, thrown and rebounding from the elbow joint, and that his whole arm made these motions from the shoulder joint. The image of overcontrolled tautness implied by the words *lifting* and *striking* and of undercontrolled flaccidity by the word *dropping* had been misleading. He consciously weeded out these images and replaced them: lifting to hit the keys became swinging to sound them; pressing weight onto keys became releasing weight into them.

Max also became aware that he was shifting his interest from the initiation of tones to their vibratory reaction, sonic as well as physical. He realized that with his exclusive focus on accurate rhythmic and dynamic arrivals, he had been hearing piano sounds mainly as entrances—"attack points"—much as one would hear the succession of key-clicks while typing. His ear was now awakening to the envelope of each sound and the singing-through of tone.

Reverberation beyond the Body's Boundaries

The reverberation of movement is a system of responsiveness that does not stop at the body's boundaries. How we allow an action to flow through ourselves determines the way we interact with people and things. Mandy, chopping wood, may bind herself, tightening muscles and locking joints so that she withdraws somewhat from the impact; or she may so loosen the action—by flopping, say, at her wrists—that her trunk and legs cannot get their force through to ax and wood. Or she may focus her whole body into the swing, and chop so that the play of her weight feeds into the act, no more or less than is just appropriate to her intention. When she shakes hands in greeting she may tighten or loosen her hand and arm in such a way that the flow of intimacy is shut out; or with reverberant movement she may allow all her joints to participate. Encounters with different people will call for different calibrations of tension.

Since reverberation allows the contact to flow back into her, Mandy can learn to register and respond to it as she breaks out of settled patterns of limitation and broadens her palette of choices. Her actions become more accurate. She feels with more discrimination the hand she is touching; she feels the wood and allows it to talk back to her through the ax.

Stephen, a piano tuner who was also a skillful musician, went to Thomas for help with chronic pain in his right fore-arm. Thomas noticed that when Stephen pulled on the tun-ing hammer he braced his elbow against the piano case and concentrated effort in his forearm. Thomas suggested that he stand with core support, free his elbow, let the joints of shoulder and arm be spacious, and distribute the action in such a way that his legs could provide power to the small pulls of the hammer. At first Stephen was afraid that he would lose refinement of control; the quality of his work de-pended on being able to move the hammer with delicacy, and full-bodied participation would seem to lack the necessary discretion. But as he experimented during the following week his forearm pain abated, and a reverberative use of his body gained him more, not less, control over the action. His sense of contact with the instrument altered; he had the impression of feeling through the hammer not just to the pin, but be-yond, into the string itself.

Habits of speaking often reveal the same non-rever-berant symptoms as habits of moving. Some speak in rushed tumbles of words and, when pausing to consider what to say next, intrude on the interval with an "uh" or "um" rather than let what has just been said echo until its meaning has collected. Others flatten into a monotone the upward and downward curves of melodic line that are natural to words and word groups; others drain accented syllables of volume and gloss them over, perhaps sharply exploding a syllable here and there as if to rev up the faltered vocal energy.

Cynthia was rehearsing the exclamation, "Listen!" The action of the play turned on this simple single line, and her director had been exasperated not only that the line could barely be heard from the auditorium but that its meaning was off: it conveyed, if anything, meekness, not the intended urgent despair. Now as she tried the word at home she noticed that the muscles on either side of her neck were taut and her jaw set. The word had to fight its way out between clenched teeth, and the resonance, except for the hiss of its middle portion, was swallowed.

She recalled Karen, the flutist, practicing a small backward swing of the head upon inhalation, then tossing her head forward to create the instrument's tone with exhalation. The parallel with speech did not escape her. She practised the release of neck muscles to permit her head to swing back a bit before she spoke and then toss its weight onto "Listen!" and she sensed the concomitant flexible yielding of her spine. The wind-up gave her access to the line's motivation, and the toss gained fullness of sound. "So this is what is meant by 'giving your words weight!'" she mused.

The fuller, clearer sound gave her something substantial to reverberate. And during the return to stillness—as she felt the actions of her head, tongue, teeth, and palate come to rest—she actually heard the word, as if she were listener as well as speaker. It occurred as an oddly fresh phenomenon: she realized that normally she did not register her own words. Touched, she had a rush of connection with the pivotal meaning of "Listen!" at that moment in the play. Later, in rehearsal, she found that as she perceived her own words she was also hearing the other actors empathically; acting became earnest. The interconnecting web spun by speech had less pretense, more reality.

Affective Gesture and Stage Fright

Actions take place in the drift of affective life: reverberation of the lifts, reaches, and turns involved in housework is tinted by the prevailing humor. But some gestures—an athlete's victorious wave upon setting a new record, a parent's fond good-bye stroke of a child's hair before she sets off to school—are in themselves emotionally weighted. As a part of their reverberation, and in order to fulfill their individuating expression, the poignancy of these gestures needs to be sensed and liberated. If you throw your arms out in a gesture of welcome to an old friend, it is not just any lifting and opening of the arms but is specific to this moment and this friend. As you make the movement, whose very shaping is determined by the complexion and history of your friendship, reverberation depends on your "being moved" by the feelings carried in the spontaneous, yet freighted, gesture. If during the gesture its apt expressiveness is censored, the very arm motion becomes awkward and the welcome stilted.

Have you had the experience of skipping or twirling about with a particular joy and then suddenly noticing someone watching? You may continue skipping, but the movement curbs itself and becomes homogenized into a generic skip. The expression of this moment's joy shrinks. Musicians and others who perform are all too well acquainted with stage fright. The daring, abandon, and depths of contact that had been present in rehearsals just a few days before flip out of reach and in their stead appears a mask of timidity, restraint, and shallowness. Excitement, by heightening tension, restricts both the performing movements and the flow of affect; the resonances one had grown accustomed to in rehearsal disappear. At best, months of preparation will have made the finely honed technical skills and the connection to the feeling-tone of the music so habitual that these can reassert themselves, even under performance pressure; as the concert goes on and the excitement focuses on the music, the playing can become increasingly reverberative, and this then launches an upward spiral of possibility. At worst, the restrictions compound themselves and the systemic tightening stifles communication; the performance is scarcely accomplished.

Self-defeating approaches to stage fright are unfortunately tempting *in media res*. If a pianist's hands are shaking, holding the wrists rigid may salvage some of the control being lost at the fingertips. But if the impulse to restrict wrist movement can be allayed and the shaking hands borne with at first, and if reverberative swings of the torso from the hip joints can be fostered, catching the player up in the rhythmic pleasures of the music, the release of weight through arms and hands will improve circulation and ease the shaking.

Reverberation as Healing

Reverberation heals. If we are at heart good-natured creatures, and if in at least one basic movement, such as walking, we experience the repleteness of reverberation, then a walk swinging through us when we are out of sorts can right us. The reverberations of our natural walk penetrate and retune us to our truer depths. John and Carla had a marriage agreement that when arguing occurred, one or both of them would take a walk. This was a lenitive that had served them over a 50-year relationship: whoever walked was usually jostled into a happier state and the argument lost its grit.

Consciously directing awareness of reverberation can heal localized musculoskeletal pain—a backache, a sprained ankle, a shoulder tendonitis. When a part of the body is in pain we characteristically immobilize it because movement hurts. The splinting mechanisms are muscular contraction, which eliminates or reduces the reverberation of an injury, and the inflammatory response, which stiffens the tissue around the injury by engorging it. If the pain is local, we are likely to go on about our business, limping or making whatever other adjustments are necessary to use the rest of ourselves with minimal disturbance of the sensitive area.

Immobilizing has its obvious short-run advantages, but over time problems may come into play. Sustained muscular contraction and engorging interfere with healing by restricting the flow of body fluids through the injured area. Whereas an ankle with reverberative movement is served by a constant stream of fresh blood and lymph, the tissue around a swollen and rigid ankle becomes sluggish and choked. Muscles which have shifted their function from movement to prevention of movement quickly habituate themselves to this self-protective task and, unless deliberately reeducated, will retain at least a trace of the altered pattern even after the need has passed. The whole body participates in these adaptations: one does not limp with an ankle but with a whole walking pattern, and it is difficult to break free from this set of limitations once it is established.

Another danger in immobilizing injuries is that adhesions are allowed to settle in; muscles that are meant to slide against one another may, if there has been an injury, catch hold so that they drag on each other, making movement crude and restricting its range or, in extreme cases, freezing it into a traffic jam of self-contradictions.

In painful situations there is an impulse to withdraw. This is part of our self-preserving makeup: a finger touches the hot stove and signals are flashed to pull it away. The long-range consequences can be detrimental; if the finger is no longer touching the stove but is still hurting, we may act as if we were trying to pull away from the finger itself. The mechanism is once again muscular contraction, and the psychological effect is disintegrative: the painful place, for all the attention it calls to itself, becomes something not quite a part of us.

You can hear the attitude in the language used: not "I hurt" but "it hurts"; "my back aches." The painful place becomes an object.

To induce reverberation deliberately is to reverse both immobilization and withdrawal and to reincorporate the injured part—to invite it to take its place once again in one's self-identity and overall pattern of movement. It might be useful to think of this process as an embrace of consciousness that penetrates, as one might hope to touch a misbehaving child, exerting an influence that does not just bump against the surface of the behavior but guides a transformation at deeper levels. The process is simple: moving at or near the point of injury and allowing the tissue to reverberate as fully as is possible without pain. We are looking for the precise range and vigor that will not stir up a contracting reaction but will elicit small, integrative waves of motion into the distressed area. Healing by reverberation calls for a level of activity which is appropriate to the particular moment and which may change from moment to moment. If the process works, if in fact healing takes place, then the appropriate level becomes a more vigorous one; if the chosen level of vigor is not quite accurate and causes a painful reaction, then the activity is to be quieted. The primary tool in this constant process of adjustment is percipience—the opposite pole from withdrawal. Heightened awareness allows one to search out the suitable movement, which in turn draws awareness deeper.

Music can guide reverberative healing and help to sustain it. If the music is quieting, it will support the intent to move with attention focused inward.

The appropriateness not only of range, quickness, and weight, but also of direction, is determined by sensory feedback from the injury itself. Pain may establish a boundary line that is much more restricted, say, in a forward reach than in a reach behind or to the side. Healing movement respects the boundary but deftly questions it, assuming that the line has some flexibility to it, some negotiability, and that it can gradually be moved if one can become sensitive enough to the nuances of response.

Sometimes it may be helpful to begin by moving a neighboring joint rather than the suffering one, closing in on the center of the problem in gradual steps. The flexing and extending of the ankle will send into a strained knee ripples of effect that may be just enough.

Since the lifting of body weight may be more challenging than the painful situation will allow, it will perhaps be necessary to invent movements that leave the injury pendant: softly swaying the torso for example, and letting responsive arm motions flow through the shoulder. Where the affliction is in a weight-bearing part of the body such as a knee or ankle, it may be useful to lie down, letting a supportive surface take the weight, and to find movements that either do not oppose gravity or that minimize the weight lifted.

Immersion of the body in water allows normal patterns of movement without the need for weight-bearing. With a sprained ankle, for instance, one can begin walking in water deep enough that one almost floats, and then day by day move into shallower water to bring more weight into play. With a shoulder problem, one can allow the arm to float upward in the water, exploring that direction of movement without having to lift the arm's weight.

Imagine that you are afflicted with shoulder bursitis which is not painful when the shoulder is still but is acutely so with normal activity. You might begin by focusing attention into the affected place and then gently initiate arm movement and feel it reverberate through the shoulder, keeping the movement small enough to avoid pain but repeatedly approaching the threshhold. Lying down, you might rock slightly from side to side, lolling, allowing the weight of your body to hang lazily so that the movement softly jostles through the tissue. Or you might flex and extend the elbow or (this will affect the shoulder more directly) rotate the arm.

In a somewhat less acute situation, you could stand and sway gently, or slide the shoulder blade in small circles, or, leaning forward, swing so that the arm oscillates passively like a pendulum. At an even more active level, if the injury grants permission, the arm might be lifted and swung about, gently exploring the limits of its range, moving in slow-motion circles or up and down and sideways as if you were conducting an orchestra. Slow music could provide shape and rhythm and a sustained context for the movement.

Passive movement, where someone else slowly and gently moves the injured part, has the advantage that there is movement without any need at all for muscular activity, so that the person being moved can fully focus on releasing protective tension. This process calls for the capacity on the part of the mover to manipulate delicately and (what may prove to be more difficult) to let the injured person dictate all the details of movement—range, pace, and direction—from a sense of what is needed. The threshhold of pain is to be approached gently, so that a withdrawal reaction will not be provoked. If the injured person is medicated with pain-killers or any other substance that reduces sensory feedback, passive movement is best undertaken only by experienced professionals.

Sometimes active, self-initiated reverberative healing movement can be undertaken preventively. Janie wakes up with a stiff neck, having wrenched it slightly the day before and then slept on her stomach, and she knows from experience that during the day it is likely to grow stiffer and sorer and to give her a week of agonized, severely limited activity. Instead of resigning herself to her fate, she puts on a record of quiet music with a steady beat and gently sways, nods, and stretches, searching for just the movements that coax her neck out of its self-gripping. With two or three 10-minute sessions of this sort during the morning, she arrives at the point where her ordinary movement can take over as the healing process—where it sends to her neck reverberative waves that continue to tease open the knot of tension.

Deliberate healing sways along the spine are comforting, stirring, and mysteriously familiar because they magnify the small, scarcely perceived, yet almost constant oscillations by which upright equilibrium is maintained. Even when apparently still, we are forever falling slightly away from center and then bobbing and swaying until the momentum plays out and another centered stillness is attained briefly, only to be toppled from again.

In a gust of wind, the single leaf trembles while the entire tree stirs in larger undulant sweeps. Reverberative movement in our bodies can build up in tiny increments to a similar plenitude of response.

Chapter 11

Phrase
Clarifying Action

I placed a jar in Tennessee,
And round it was, upon a hill.
It made the slovenly wilderness
Surround that hill.

The wilderness rose up to it,
And sprawled around, no longer wild.
The jar was round upon the ground
And tall and of a port in air.

It took dominion everywhere.
The jar was gray and bare.
It did not give of bird or bush,
Like nothing else in Tennessee.
          Wallace Stevens,
          Anecdote of the Jar, 1957, 76

Phrasing as Personal Style

We are constantly phrasing. With or without conscious attention, we begin, accomplish, and end actions. Now and again

a phrase happens with stunning aptness—the first theme of a symphony played to perfection by the oboist, an adroit weave maneuvered through a freeway bottleneck, the punchline of a joke delivered just so. On these occasions, skill as well as intention and care have bubbled up and become accessible so that the rendering is unhampered. We are reminded how phrasing can shape time into crystalline units which are full and purposive, without either hurry or drag. Just as the "slovenly wilderness" was invited by the jar's presence to "surround that hill," the sea of confused, half-baked, or overdone actions basks in the reflected orderliness of an elegant phrase, its clear temporal shape glowing as a beacon of possibility in their midst.

Habits of phrasing play a part in the styles by which we recognize one another. Some people are predictably indecisive about starting up activities. Some are easily distracted or change horses in midstream; some do several things at once. Aunt Marion's family knows from experience what to expect of her if she calls to say she has decided to redecorate the den. The very next day finds her stripping the wallpaper and removing the furniture; but no one is surprised five weeks later when the room, still pulled apart, has made little further progress and Marion is chattering enthusiastically about acquiring a real estate license. Nor is it unexpected that the den is restored to its former appearance months later by Mr. Williams, who plods straightforwardly from assignment to accomplishment and gets the job done.

One's style of beginning, giving definition, and ending will render itself in both large and small contexts. How we bring relationships to a close, or finish a day's work, will be similar to the way we conclude a technical report or put the lawn mower back in the garage. Aunt Marion's sentences often begin with a burst, wander into a maze of competing ideas, and then peter out. She can be counted on to lose track of even such a concise action as draining water from the vegetables, interrupting herself repeatedly to peer out the kitchen window at the sparrows and to chat with the children. Meals at her house are often cool and overcooked.

The Breath as Phrase

Breathing is an organic experience of phrasing. Each breath is a phrase, and illustrates the sequence through which any phrase moves:

Beginning

Rising action (inhalation)

Climax

Falling action (exhalation)

End

Juncture

A healthy individual sitting quietly in balance moves through the phrase of a single breath something like this: from stillness—juncture—comes inhalation. Its beginning, though not abrupt, is distinct. The rising action of inhalation is an easy chest-billowing sweep of expansion up, hovering, and just over a peak of climax which defines the extent of the inhaling sweep and embraces its full spread. After the climax the quality of movement changes: away-from becomes back-toward. The outward swell of the chest diminishes inward as the falling action of exhalation streams irreversibly, slides, and empties back into the stillness of the juncture between breaths.

The next breath, and the next, while maintaining the same outline, will show differences: the climax perhaps broader in scope, the exhalation slower, the juncture deeper or quicker. If the person stands up and begins to run, the rhythm of successive events will change dramatically but the sequence will remain.

Hierarchy in Phrasing

Phrasing, like human structure, is hierarchical: shorter phrases nest themselves into larger ones. A step out the door is absorbed into the many-stepped walk to a neighbor's house, and that longer phrase into the still longer one of paying a visit. A life from birth to death may be sensed as a single long phrase or as a tiny subphrase in the history of the world. The level of complexity at which we choose to keep our intentions clear has much to do with how well we navigate our lives.

Marion's distractibility is a problem of allowing herself to focus too exclusively on moment-by-moment details; being so involved with each of the steps, she loses track of where they are meant to take her. She can improve the quality of her doings by increasing awareness of the larger units (higher in the hierarchy of nested phrases)—for example, by putting the particular moment of draining the vegetables distinctly into its context of getting dinner on the table. The acting teacher Stanislavski called this process "sticking to the channel."

> A certain pilot was asked how he could ever remember, over a long stretch, all the minute details of a coast with its turns, shallows and reefs. He replied: "I am not concerned with them; *I stick to the channel.*" (Stanislavski 1936, 107)

The channel is the level in the hierarchy of nested phrases—the level of complexity—that is best held in the foreground of consciousness. In a walk to the neighbor's house barefoot over a rocky terrain strewn with broken glass, the short phrases made by each footstep would be an appropriate focus. Were the way a dependable grassy stretch, the long phrase (the visit as a whole) could best be the channel. Mr. Williams, who puts Marion's den back in order, is her opposite in phrasing style, his individual actions so oriented to getting the job done that the smaller, nested phrases of color choice, painting, and papering lack the care that could make the result unique and the execution joyful.

Contemporary culture encourages a pendulum swing between opposite styles of phrasing. On one hand, many of us are driven by the work ethic of long-range goals, deferred satisfactions, the "bottom line." This is Mr. Williams's working style: smaller phrases lose clarity and shape in the sweeping current of the larger purpose. On the other hand, recreation is often organized in short bursts of activity for immediate gratification and lacks the satisfaction of sustained interest. "Be here now" schools of thought, reacting against the sterility of a business approach to life, sometimes encourage the abandonment of longer phrases of intention. Thomas Hardy studied the psychology of exclusive presentness in the character of Sergeant Troy:

> He was a man to whom memories were an encumbrance, and anticipations a superfluity. Simply feeling, considering, and caring for what was before his eyes, he was vulnerable only in the present. His outlook upon time was as a transient flash of the eye now and then: that projection of consciousness into days gone by and to come, which makes the past a synonym for the pathetic and the future a word for circumspection, was foreign to Troy. (Hardy [1897] 1918, 190)

If one keeps in mind the hierarchical nature of phrase, conscious shaping of units of action will lead not to exaggeration of one level at the expense of others but, on the contrary, to that combination of immediate inspiration with sustained intention that marks great endeavors of all kinds; it will make keen one's participation with *now*, and also intensify the relationship to past and future.

The bassoonist Lisa one day stood outside a room at the conservatory and listened to a pianist practicing. Having read an article about "performance phrase," the level of phrasing at which one's attention is best focused in order to organize all other levels (Alexandra Pierce 1982, 26–46), she was curious whether she could hear the level on which this pianist was centered. Repetition told the story: the music would move along until a troublesome spot arrived; the pianist would stop, back up a few notes, and repeat the spot until it was smoothly executed and musically interesting. When a longer section of music was played through without stops, Lisa could still hear this preoccupation with tiny units: there were flashes of brilliance, but they did not hang together with one another; longer phrases, and the yet longer ones into which they nested, were not played with a feeling for their shapes. The music lacked intelligence, though Lisa knew the pianist to be a discerning person.

Down the hall she heard Harold practicing a trumpet concerto, and she stopped to listen again. Here was the opposite extreme: Harold's repetitions took in pages and pages of music, often a whole movement. Themes, their variations and contrasting ideas, were run through indiscriminately, so that their distinctive features were unable to play off one another. There was a generalized build of intensity and a denouement over long sections, but the notes and shorter phrases were so lost within the larger shapes that they had little life of their own.

Beginning and Ending

By changing her style of phrasing, Aunt Marion can improve the effectiveness of nearly everything she does. Her present phrasing style is, however, one of the tools she will necessarily use in this transformative process, and she can therefore expect to be somewhat inefficient, particularly at the beginning. She will probably get lost in the very process of examining how she gets lost in phrases, and though she needs to put her short phrases (draining the vegetables) into their larger contexts (serving dinner), she can also profit from a study of phrases that are small enough for her to grasp in their totality. Here, habit will be less likely to undo her efforts.

Reading a book that a moment ago was lying on her desk, Marion has an edgy feeling of having gone astray. The book is in her hand; she is not very clear how it got there and has even forgotten why she picked it up in the first place. Oh, yes, it was on top of some papers she was planning to grade. She decides to take a moment to study her phrasing. The goal of the phrase had been to move the obstructing book to a new location: not to read it, not to see whether it was overdue at the library.

Of course, a phrase may legitimately change direction in midflight to other options. The succession of actions through a day is in good part improvisatory. We set out to accomplish a certain task, but other possibilities crop up and beckon while we are under way, so we detour or redefine the task in order to follow impulses which on the spur of the moment are judged promising. A path through the day is created whose twists and turns are evident in hindsight but could not have been predicted.

Underlying intentions also need to shift and keep pace. When Marion started to read the book, she was thwarting the original intention to grade the papers, and she became vaguely uneasy, felt pressed for time, and read without focus. To avoid these common symptoms of the poor-phrasing malady, she can recast her intentions so that reading the book becomes the new purpose (the papers beneath will be attended to later); or she can hold firm to the original intention while permitting a subsidiary excursion into reading for a bit. The diversionary phrase of book reading then nests within the larger phrase, whose purpose remains steady.

Marion realizes that the channel for the morning is to grade the essays from her American literature students. The phrase whose movement is under view, shifting the book, is subordinate to that larger purpose, and she decides not to allow further ornamenting phrases to develop: no reading in the book, no looking to see whether it is overdue. She will deflect only for this momentary study of the phrase itself. Purposes which had been vaguely operant are now openly chosen and the capacity for self-discipline can be tapped, giving her a sense of relief, not restriction.

Next she turns her attention to the sequence of parts within the shifting-the-book phrase and realizes that she had begun to shift the book quite without notice; no wonder she had gotten lost in midflight. She decides to explore the temporal boundaries of this phrase: its very initiation, and then its ending. She waits to begin until she has become still, and she is surprised to find that to do this requires considerable concentration. She notices several random small motions that do not seem pertinent to the moment but which form a continuous jittery backdrop: rubbing her neck, running her hand through her hair, a bemused smile left over from the telephone chat just finished. As she observes and amiably wills herself motionless, these off-the-point movements settle with little resistance. The stillness is refreshing. It is time to begin the phrase, shifting-the-book-from-the-papers; she marks the instant by saying, "Begin!" The distinction between stillness and motion is clean-cut, lends vigor to the movement, and aims it clearly toward accomplishment and completion.

She goes through a similar process with the end of the phrase. When the book has been set down, she lets the action reverberate and then punctuates by saying, "End!" As with the beginning, it takes a conscious effort to unclutter this phrase–border, but when achieved, the conciseness of finishing pleases her and once again grants unaccustomed access to stillness.

Performed with clarified initiation and completion, which have lent heightened perception of its function (to clear the way for paper grading), the movement has acquired shapeliness and character. The contour of its linear tracing through the air becomes almost visible: up from the papers and over to the right to rest down on a bare spot of the desk. The climactic moment of lift-off, which brings to mind the springing of a deer, has a special intensity while the remainder of the phrase organizes itself as a spun-out denouement. This phrase which at first notice had been both haphazard and commonplace now gives off a glimmer of emotional tone. The book, after all, is one Marion looks forward to. The gesture of lifting to put it aside is sternly abrupt (rendering, as it does, "I won't take time for you now"), yet it also reveals a bond, especially apparent as the book is put down: present denial of the book's charms is reluctant and will be temporary ("I'll arrange a later time, just for you"). The purposiveness of the phrase allows the expression of this rich background.

Arcing the Aesthetic Qualities of Phrase

Beginning, rising action, climax, falling action, ending, and juncture: these, the parts of a phrase, the generic ordering of the narrative curve, can be experienced kinesthetically through the gesture of an arc drawn in the air with your arm. Begin with (or imagine beginning with) your hand resting on your thigh; with a slight forward swing of your torso to initiate movement, lift the arm to trace with deliberation a narrow arc, up above the level of your head, then down to a point of rest on the other thigh. The effort of lifting weight up and over the peak of the arc gives a kinesthetic sense of action rising into climax; a controlled return to the thigh reveals falling action as a measured release into juncture.

One level of phrasing is made evident in *The Anecdote of the Jar* by the poem's arrangement into lines:

> I placed a jar in Tennessee,
> And round it was, upon a hill.
> It made the slovenly wilderness
> Surround that hill.

These four line-phrases nest into two longer phrases, both of which are sentences. The two sentences nest into the stanza, and the stanza into the whole poem.

You can amplify your sense of the lines as phrases by speaking them and at the same time drawing an arc through the air for each line, in such a way that speaking and moving are inseparably linked. You will probably notice that your manner of speaking the lines is enhanced: their coherence becomes demonstrable in the accompanying arcs.

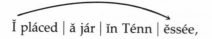

Ĭ pláced | ă jár | ĭn Ténn | ĕssée,   phrase motion
    iambic meter

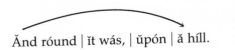

phrase motion

Ănd róund | ĭt wás, | ŭpón | ă híll.   iambic meter

The singleness of each line-phrase is superimposed upon a meter which divides the line into four iambic feet. Each phrase-line, overriding the metric units, connects word meanings so that the thought is apparent. Without a clear sense of phrase, the singsonginess of meter may rule, perhaps more crudely accentuated than necessary—I placed a jar in Tennessee—and this can disconnect the thought. There is ebullience in the tension between phrase unity and metrical substructure as they coexist.

If you next draw a single arc for the first sentence and another arc for the second sentence, you can hear clearly the individual lines nested within the sentences and the meter within the lines. And so on: make a single arc for each stanza, and finally one for the whole poem. If another person is interested, you can each arc a different level simultaneously: one of you, for example, the separate lines and the other the two-line sentences, so that each of you can experience one level visually and the other level kinesthetically.

By analyzing the nested hierarchy of phrases and actively expressing phrases with arcing, you reveal the articulation of the structure, including irregularities that give the work its character. For instance, the single line "And round it was, upon a hill" falls into two shorter phrases—it has a level in the hierarchy that is not present in the lines around it. On the other hand, the two lines "It made the slovenly wilderness/ Surround that hill" hang together as a single phrase more strongly than they break into two units.

Climax

The search for climax is a search for meaning. Organizing the parts of a phrase around a node of intensity specifies and illuminates intention. The line "I placed a jar in Tennessee," for instance, can find its climactic emphasis on any of the words, and each choice results in a different meaning and tone of voice:

<u>I</u> placed a jar in Tennessee	not anyone else
I <u>placed</u> a jar in Tennessee	there was deliberation in the act
I placed <u>a</u> jar in Tennessee	just one
I placed a <u>jar</u> in Tennessee	this particular thing
I placed a jar <u>in</u> Tennessee	not outside or on the border
I placed a jar in <u>Tennessee</u>	not in Kentucky

Not only the location but the intensity of climax is variable. If "jar" is the appropriate climax of this line, it does not in the context of the stanza call for an outburst (which would subordinate the rising and falling parts of the phrase too strongly); a graph of the line's energy makes more sense when it looks like a foothill rather than like Mt. Fuji, because the line-phrase (with its mild climax) functions as rising action for the two-line phrase which climaxes on "round."

In both the analysis and the performance of temporal works, attention to phrase shape—which is initially a matter of locating beginnings and endings, and then of shaping climaxes—pays rich dividends. It unravels the meaning of scripts, choreographies, and scores, and therefore gives performers the blessing and security of understanding: at each moment they know where they are in the whole structure of the work and can give their commitment to the present; they can "be here now" not in the arbitrary manner of Sergeant Troy but with an intelligent grasp of how past and future are gathered into this instant (see Roger Pierce, "Three Play Analyses," 1969).

Weary of productions where actors deliver speeches with only a hazy understanding of how they are meant to function in the play, Oscar decided that in directing Pinter's *The Homecoming*—a difficult but meticulously constructed play—he would spend a significant portion of the allotted rehearsal time examining phrase structure with the cast. The level of performance phrase would be the French scene, a unit of action whose boundaries are marked off by the entrance or exit of characters. With the cast he located the climax of each French scene and then delineated both the smaller nested phrases and the larger groupings—the phrases that gathered together the French scenes. The play was thus explored with the actors until the action of each phrase, and of each character within that phrase, was understood.

Although Oscar became a little nervous as the scheduled days of rehearsal passed with the cast still engaged in this formal study of the play, the final result in quality of performance was spectacular. A basic sense that "we know what we are doing" pervaded the production and gave even the less experienced actors a seasoned air. Oscar was particularly impressed at how characterization was enriched. The actress playing Ruth, for instance, first approached her role with the question "What is Ruth like?" She came up with a sensitive answer, but her early work on the role was one-dimensional and boring because she was acting her image of the character with such consistency. The study of phrase and climax changed the question to "What is Ruth doing at this moment, and how does this moment express what she is doing in the rest of the scene and in the whole play?" Divergences, contra-dictions, and sudden shifts—even in midsentence—began to emerge. These dramatic surprises did not throw the characterization or the play off the track because the relationship between the moment and the totality had been thoroughly digested through all the levels of phrasing hierarchy. Character grew into a three-dimensional weave of contrasting strands.

In discussing his discoveries with theater colleagues and with musician and dancer friends, Oscar found that phrase and climax were not generally given sufficient attention by performers or directors. Lingering over text or score, the application of wit needed to ferret out the accurate intensity shape—that is, the *meaning*—of phrases was, in the press of time, surprisingly neglected. One colleague argued that climax best emerged on its own, pushed forward in performance by unanalyzable forces within the piece; a musician friend feared that establishing a single climax within a phrase would oversimplify and cut off ambiguities that give depth. Oscar's experience was that phrases with unclear climax are not rich in their ambiguity but limp, impoverished, and helpless; they crumble apart rather than form intelligible, energetic groupings.

In verbal works—plays, poems, speeches, conversations—the most noticeable yield from a clarification of climax is usually semantic: phrase shape delivers meaning. In the phrases of daily movement life, the issue is likely to be effectiveness, with the question of meaning lurking in the background. Annette, 86 years old, understood the principle of collecting and then tossing the weight of her head and trunk forward to stand up. But with increasing frailty she was finding it ever more difficult to get up from her favorite chair, in part because she acted hesitantly; her vagueness often resulted in failure and left her struggling to push herself up against the chair arms. She found it a substantial help to make her purpose clear to herself (we might say she clarified the *meaning* of the movement) by fashioning the phrase around its climax. When she wished to stand up she would first picture the action as a phrase that would climax when her weight had been thrown forward and, balanced over her feet, she was beginning to thrust herself upward. Having visualized the action, she would then launch into it, and to catch the climax would vocalize a firm "Up!" at the moment of lift. After a few weeks of practice, this manner of getting out of the chair had become a familiar ritual which was adapting itself to other actions: standing up from the toilet, arising from her bed in the morning, lifting dishes from the coffee table, straightening up after tying her shoes. The zip and certainty at these moments that were scattered throughout the day regained for Annette a measure of her youthful spryness.

Watching the Olympics one day, she was intrigued to see how similar the training of a pole vaulter must have been to her own work with climax. Every prior move led carefully to the concentrated moment of push-off from the top of the pole, and the initiating juncture—before he began running—was filled with a quiet marshaling of intention. Runners obviously paced themselves with consciousness of phrase shape of the whole race and of the need to build it to a definite climax, even though that phrase was in part improvisational.

A good opportunity for experimenting with climax is offered by repetitive movements such as brushing a dog or washing a window. As Marion swept leaves off the sidewalk, she noticed how differently phrased the broom-strokes were from those she had used a few minutes earlier when she was sweeping the bedroom floor. The motivation was different:

where now she was flinging the leaves outward to fall where they might, inside she had been drawing tufts of dust toward her and at the same time trying to prevent them from floating away. Climax had occurred near the beginning of each stroke when the broom, with bristles holding to the floor, first penned in the dust. Outside, in leaf sweeping, climax occurred near the end of each stroke, after the leaves had been brushed along and just as the broom pushed up from the sidewalk to send them flying. As she continued to sweep away the leaves, she deliberately gave herself over to the "off the sidewalk" purpose of each stroke; climax found its full force as she continued to yield weight through the brushing part of each stroke and allowed the maximum toned stretch in her trunk as the broom lifted from the sidewalk. The sweeping took on a playful fervor not usual for her when she was doing chores.

Juncture

> . . . for lo, the eternal and sovereign luminous space,
> where rule the unnumbered stars,
> is the air we breathe out.
> And in the moment betwixt the breathing in
> and the breathing out
> is hidden all the mysteries
> of the Infinite Garden.
> > *Essene Gospel of Peace*

Climax and juncture are opposites. Climax is the peak of intensity which binds together the phrase and individualizes its meaning; juncture, the cessation of one action and the birth of the next, articulates the distinction between phrases with interludes of stillness.

Religions and spiritual disciplines share a vision of human nature, and of reality itself, as essentially quiet. Emptiness, Nirvana, "the peace that passeth all understanding," "the still, small voice"—these and other descriptions of divine quiescence are often depicted as the creative source of activity. Maturation and deepening are pursued through the nonaction of meditation or prayer, which penetrate the surface of busy-ness in order to reach the quiet within it. Just as music arises from and returns to silence, as painting takes place on a blank canvas and dance on an empty stage, life enacts itself on a background of personal and cosmic quiet.

Actors in Japanese Noh theater focus their attention on this negative quality, which they call *ma*. Noh acting "is a matter of doing just enough to create the *ma* that is blank space-time where nothing is done. . . . *Ma* is the core of the expression, where the true interest lies (Komparu, cited in Pilgrim 1986, 259; see Alexandra Pierce 1987 for a discussion of juncture in musical performance). Though musicians and actors in the West usually do not work so deliberately with this quality of rest between phrases, it is known and is sometimes referred to as "breathing."

It has been conjectured that human culture is increasingly and perilously noisy because we have come to mistrust and fear silence and to associate it with death, which in turn is not felt to be a natural event (Schafer 1977, 256). As children we are often required to be still in violation of our natural rhythms: to sit at one's first-grade desk for hours when muscles are crying out for activity can make quietness a painful affair. Our evolving technology emphasizes speed; we think of life in terms of accomplishments. Yet a shift of mind can suggest that life *is* stillness—that our flurried doings, emerging from the depths, are its overtones. An awareness of juncture, even in seemingly trivial actions, carries the potential for tapping into our interior of stillness so that we can allow it to penetrate into the flow of consciousness from one doing to another.

There are two ways to mistreat junctures. One is to neglect them: to scurry so that the end of one phrase and the beginning of the next are blurred together. Another is to fill them with extraneous jitters, which frequently develop a life of their own and become new phrases, unintended and off the point, and hold us away from the refreshment of genuine rest. Thomas dealt with the second of these juncture problems in movement awareness class by inviting the students to experience phrase and juncture as a headnote to whatever else was planned for the day's meeting. Having made a large circle and found standing balance, they held hands, closed their eyes, quieted themselves, and waited to receive a squeeze in one hand and pass it along through the other. The peak of intensity in the squeeze was the climax, after which, one by one around the circle, they slowly released hands and entered upon juncture. Here followed a rich laboratory for observation: though they knew the stillness would be brief, the students found themselves dodging it by numerous techniques that they came to acknowledge as familiar patterns: wiggling their fingers, strumming their thighs, curling and uncurling toes, rocking, tapping, scratching, adjusting clothes or hair, starting up an idle conversation.

Over the semester they learned to release this nervous reaction to juncture: during its moment they consciously maintained standing balance and concentrated on a release of weight in the face, arms, hands, legs, feet. At first, many felt odd; the stillness radiated with the energy of the just-finished phrase which had gathered them into the circle. Because this alert quiet was expressive, students felt exposed, as if they might seem too cooperative and engaged, or absorbed in prayer. However, the sense of composure gradually overcame the strangeness, and they realized that the mannered clutter between phrases had been a mask for self-consciousness, a vent for anxiety or fatigue, or a well-practiced expression of diffidence toward their education.

Once these extraneous movements were perceived, to track them through the fabric of the day and ease into the stillness earned by actions became a satisfying discipline. Some of the students went further and focused on clutter during pauses in their speaking. Such habits as tossing the hair back or clearing the throat could be set to rout with a little diligence, but it was more of a challenge to become conscious of how frequently they filled the junctures in speech with such sound-jitters as "um," "uh," "you know," "see what I mean?" Few of them could utter many sentences in succession without the occurrence of these fillers. It was obviously easier to hear and understand someone whose speech included moments of silence, where the listener could rest, reflect, and allow thought to be moved along on the next wave of words. To alter the habit of filling pauses with unneeded sounds took a desire to coexist equably with listeners—not to pull on them with the choke-chain of an "uh" while the next thought was hurriedly being formed into speakable words, but to grant their patience and their willingness to hear through to the end.

As the element of discontinuity between discrete actions, juncture does not necessarily take place in time; one action may follow immediately upon another or they may overlap, as often occurs in music. A receptionist who finds that she must simultaneously greet three customers and answer two telephone calls can contribute to her own and her customers' sanity if she suspends each of these intertwined, counterpointing events in a separate mental compartment and does not allow them to run together into a single overwhelming phrase. Suppose she decides to put the second caller on hold, suspending that phrase across the time span she will take to transact other business before she returns to it. If she chops off the end of the putting-on-hold subphrase (which is to receive its full juncture only when she returns to the call), and gives it no element of momentary completion, she is likely to face three separate problems: she may offend the caller by her brusqueness, she may not quite free her own attention for the intervening phrase, and she may have difficulty making instantaneous reentry into the suspended phrase. Both she and the caller need to be allowed to touch into the quiet that weaves this action into the flow of events and that promises a fuller completion in the course of time.

She need not, as we have said, give any *time* to this partial completion; she has none to spare. What she gives is reverberation, a response to the event that has just occurred which expresses that she has been truly engaged and has not already jumped ahead to the next. Juncture is the moment for reverberation, for one phrase to settle into itself, to follow through with whatever completion is appropriate to the flow of events. In this realm of reflection the next phrase gathers itself for launch.

Lisa's teachers had often told her that her bassoon playing sounded restless. As she began to pay careful attention to phrasing, she noticed how often she cut short concluding gestures; at the ends of phrases she would characteristically hurry to set her fingers in position for the next phrase so as to be ready ahead of time. Then she would wait. The new hand position was not a juncture that reverberated the previous phrase, but one that resulted from the hand shift: this maneuver had become a phrase in itself, outside the music and confusing it.

With this discovery in mind, she practiced a particular passage where a difficult shift of hand position was required, and found that if she stayed to reverberate the end of the old phrase, she could move accurately to the next position precisely on the impulse of beginning the new phrase. She disciplined herself to entertain this musical rather than mechanical stillness, and the improvement in sound was quite remarkable. The preceding phrase became fulsome and articulate, and the succeeding phrase was initiated with vitality.

One evening Lisa was in the audience of an orchestra concert. Before the finish of the last chord of Beethoven's Fifth Symphony she had gathered her gloves and coat in readiness; during the applause she squeezed her way down the row to the aisle. The time saved was insignificant, she later realized ruefully. She had not let Beethoven's long coda reach its triumphant conclusion, had not respected the neighboring audience, had not expressed her appreciation to the orchestra. To be a little ahead of the game was a consistent pattern in her phrasing-life.

Giving attention to juncture allows us to come home to ourselves and is therefore an antidote to harried living. At a practical level, giving special attention to the ends of actions can prevent a burdensome accumulation of incompletions. Or since many of a day's tasks must be suspended before they reach full closure, one can find the style and degree of partial completion that will allow a phrase to sit comfortably on the shelf while attention is turned elsewhere. On a specifically interpersonal level, much unhappiness that arises between people can be described as "unfinished business," one sign of which is a lack of peace. Jesus speaks to the point:

> If thou bring thy gift to the altar, and there rememberest
> that thy brother hath aught against thee; leave there thy

> gift before the altar, and go thy way; first be reconciled
> to thy brother, and then come and offer thy gift. (Mat-
> thew 5: 23–24)

A daily time for meditation, prayer, reflection, or journal writing creates a juncture, just as the sabbath was meant to be not simply a vacation (a new phrase of its own) but the week's juncture, and New Year's Day—or Christmas or Easter or a birthday—the moment for stepping back to take a larger perspective on a year, that is, to allow it to reverberate. At all levels of phrasing, juncture serves this contextualizing purpose.

Phrasing as a Principle of Movement

Just as balance, weight release, and reverberation are principles of natural movement in space, clear and shapely phrasing is our *temporal* birthright in enacting purpose and meaning. "Everything that he did had the clean, simple lines that come of integrity and generosity," says George Dennison of one of his characters in *Luisa Domic* (1985, 31). Where intention (even if improvisational) is without self-contradiction, clarity of phrase will show itself in the expansive flow of body weight thrown off the vertical axis into a climax and then gathered once again into relative rest.

Imagine this idealized rendering of an ordinary phrase: Aunt Marion answers the telephone while she sits at her desk. The intention to reach initiates the phrase with a forward swing of trunk and head weight, extended by the reaching arm and supported by sitting bones and feet. A reverberating span of tissue spreads out from the spine to the periphery of the gesture, leading into the climax—the hand's contact with the receiver. The reception of off-balance weight by the supportive parts of the body (particularly the feet against the floor) sets up the return to balanced sitting, whereupon the action reverberates into juncture: the hand seems to settle, as if to assume the phone's shape; the coolness and texture of that surface meet awareness; small increments of coming to rest are felt in the arm and throughout the body. The impulse to speak arises from a state of balanced ease.

To contrast this spanned phrase with a less ideal one, suppose that Marion is settled onto the back of her pelvis so that her upper body is compressed over the organs. When the telephone rings and the reaching phrase begins, her hips remain relatively immobile and her legs and feet are not actively engaged in support; the swing forward then further compresses spine and organs, and she pulls her head back, withholding its potential momentum. Shoulders tighten upward into the neck. Lack of core support, isolating the phrase and its climax in the shoulder girdle, results in a jerky and disconnected phrase because the pathway from juncture to climax is freighted with a clutter of self-contradiction (immobile pelvis, compressed spine, tensed shoulders and arms, retracted head). The climax itself is overdone—the hand bumps against the receiver and grasps it tightly so that sensory feedback is obstructed—and the ending juncture fails to emerge clearly because the muscular commitment of the phrase is not fully released. A residue of this reaching phrase therefore spills over into the next phrase. "Tension"—the overdoing that results from ineffective self-support—has overridden the points of articulation between phrases.

Lack of full physical commitment expresses a withholding attitude, and Marion's underlying peacefulness—in Dennison's phrase, her integrity and generosity, which could ground the action in her psychical depths and also reflect her larger intentions—is not tapped. To load a trivial 2-second movement with such a multilayered analysis may seem a *reductio ad absurdum,* but the pattern of the movement and its phrasing will, since this is settled habit, permeate all of life. Aunt Marion, if she continues to explore the shapes of her phrases, will discover that getting lost in the middle of an action bears a direct relationship to the way she balances and supports herself, and that an efficient organization of her movement will make her body perceptibly responsive to her intentions—in other words, phrases will also be tellingly organized.

The direct relationship of phrasing style to movement style can be tested by again arcing the phrases of the first stanza of *The Anecdote of the Jar.* If, sitting, the trunk is resting on a balanced pelvis with feet supporting, head poised, chest open, and shoulders relaxed, then the phrases can be arced not just by isolated arm movements but with the participation of the whole body—from supportive feet to swinging head to arcing hand. The perception of phrase is intensified, a subtle response to the nuances of particular climactic and junctural shapes is possible, power is generated, and fuller resting is permitted.

Thomas was working one day with Lisa on the phrasing of her bassoon playing. Arcing with core-supported arm movements, she had given climaxes and junctures their precise location, shape, and intensity; she had made these choices and then experienced their full-bodied movement, and the result was exhilarating when she took them back to her instrument and translated them into sound. Clear articulation favored the play of musical ideas, and it was easy to hear one idea repeating, varying, or contrasting with another.

Lisa wanted to extend the lesson to everyday activity, so

she and Thomas planned out four simple movement phrases: from sitting, she would (1) stand up and walk to a basket of pebbles on a table in the center of the room, (2) reach into the basket, pick up one of the pebbles, and move it to another basket on the table, (3) turn and walk back to her chair, and then (4) turn and sit. To Bach's *Air on the G String* with its slow and steady bass, Lisa practiced the sequence over and over. Moving *through* the beat, not *to* it, she allowed the musical phrases to guide her movement phrases.

When she anticipated the beginnings of phrases, or when a climax was flabby or a juncture not fully articulated, the music let her know. She found herself, for example, starting to reach out for the pebble in the middle of her walk toward the basket; or she would sit down in a rush and then have to wait for the next musical cue. But gradually there arose sustained, spread phrases with everything done in its own good time—movements that looked and felt as eloquent as Bach's music. In the weeks and months that followed, Lisa would now and then repeat this formal process, and she would find herself remembering it in the midst of practical doings: about to fold up a blanket, or open the car door, or sign her name on a check, she would recall the feel of phrase beautifully rendered. She could then, with a flick of purpose, transpose that resource into the present activity. She also enjoyed turning phrase consciousness onto the deeply grooved rituals that repeat from day to day—walking outside to pick up the morning paper, setting the table, watering the house plants. She had often treated such rituals indistinctly, the phrases strung together like run-on sentences and the time spent on them unrelished. As Lisa explored their articulations and allowed them to arc fully between reverberative junctures and expressive climaxes, they became toned with affect; commonplace moments of reaching, walking, bending even took on a poetic, generic quality. She was reminded of a passage from Rilke's *Ninth Duino Elegy*:

> show him [the angel]
> the simple thing, formed from generation to generation,
> which lives as our own, at hand and within view.
> Speak to him of the things. He will stand more aston-
>   ished, as you stood
> by the rope-maker in Rome or by the potter on the Nile.

The Breath Phrase

Breathing reveals the intimate interplay between phras-ing, movement, and psychological state. Andy expresses chronic depression by dropping the weight of his head and shoulders forward over his slumped rib cage and laboring for inhalation into an indecisive climax. He exhales with an al-most-audible long sigh, and the juncture seems to have little energy for generating the next breath. In contrast with Andy's droop, Max's arrogant insecurity is embodied in the high carriage of his thorax, pulled up and held by force of back, shoulder, and neck musculature. His breathing, like his thorax and its muscular fabric, is high and short: the muscles have such a strong prior commitment to holding up unsup-ported weight that they cannot fully participate with the di-aphragm in breathing. Inhalation is quick, almost panicky, as if fearfully anticipating the "not enough" feeling of climax. Juncture is hurried, shallow: there is perhaps an unconscious reluctance to release the breath fully because the next will be so unsatisfying. In Fritz Perls's image, Max does not empty the bucket before trying to fill it again. The attempt to over-come this complex situation by conscious manipulation of the breath would probably be frustrating. Enforced changes would remain only as long as they were consciously willed, and would not be satisfying because they would fail to engage the deep reflexive levels of the nervous system.

In a balanced body, breathing phrases flow with fullness between the poles of climax and juncture; in an unbalanced body, breathing is obstructed. Given this direct relationship between stature and breathing, the breath pattern can serve as a sensitive biofeedback device that reads out the postural pattern and its implicit meaning. Attending to the breath is thus a twofold means for allowing one's background of peace to penetrate into the foreground: it directly induces fuller phrasing of the breath, and it brings postural obstructions to light and creates the occasion for gently removing them.

One widely practiced way to avail oneself of this opportunity is to follow the breath as it moves from juncture to climax to juncture, not in order to control but simply to maintain focus. This specialized form of sensory awareness brings out the inherent order and fullness of breathing, as if the more superficial, willful, self-confirming levels of the nervous system, by investing themselves in the functioning of deeper levels, learn how to step aside. Or we might say that conscious attention, in penetrating, tasting, and enjoying the peaceful quality of juncture, releases that quality of quiet to undergird and inform the entire breath-phrase. The bucket gets emptied, and then it can be filled.

Another value in breathing meditation is to illuminate the psychological pattern that lies behind disturbances in breathing: to see one's psychological behavior as chosen and to examine the values implicit in the choice. Since posture is an ever-present expression of values, the search for an easy, released balance is a simple and direct challenge to engrained habits, and meditation teachers almost universally insist on the importance of erect posture. Suzuki Roshi, as Nicki noted, goes so far as to say that erect posture *is* enlightenment.

Max now meditates daily, with a focus on his breathing. He does not encourage himself to interfere with its unconscious functioning but he deliberately experiments with the way he sits; sometimes he also stands or walks slowly while meditating. Occasionally, anxiety surfaces and Max's breathing becomes again higher in his chest, the excursions again shorter, but if he persists with sensory observation, his breath-phrases usually fill out, he finds a wellspring of peace, and the exercise becomes wordless prayer. Junctures are of particular importance: if he acquiesces in these moments of release, his breathing deepens in response, his self-image softens, and his overassertive stance melts into a more natural expression. The ordering and calming influence of this intimate experience of phrasing is refreshment to his music and to the rest of his life.

Chapter 12

Deftness

Moral reform is the effort to throw off sleep. . . . I know
of no more encouraging fact than the unquestionable
ability of man to elevate his life by a conscious endeavor.
Henry David Thoreau, *Walden* (1854) 1962, 172

Deftness and Sloth

Deftness is the nimble play of the body's periphery, the quality of its handling, footwork and speaking. Like the purling
aesthetic surface of a symphony—the tumbling of notes one
after another manifesting the deeper contrapuntal background—deftness is the precision with which we make contact as fingers grasp a spoon, footsteps meet the pavement
with delicate shifts of direction to maneuver us through a
crowded street, or tongue meets palate, teeth, and lips to

form consonants. In common with others of the animal kingdom, we humans can adapt to our environment with subtle exactitude and carry out intentions meticulously. Deftness in a surgeon or a quarterback may be given lavish social rewards and its felt lack may, as in Charlie's sense of his own clumsiness, be a lifelong source of anguish.

Certain actions call for us to muster deftness consciously: pouring boiling water from a pan into a cup, for example, or threading a needle, or crossing a swift-moving stream by hopping on rocks. We can feel the body organize itself around the upcoming event, girding itself in readiness. If this preparation is overly excited we may be surprised to find that excessive muscular tension has disrupted control of the action—that the hot water has splashed over the cup's edge, the foot has slipped into the stream.

But usually action is less exacting in its demands for deftness. We can get along in the social and natural environment well enough with a generalized aim and an approximation of contact. A friendly "Good morning! How are you?" to a neighbor will probably be understood even if it sounds more like "Mawnihrya?" Though we may often pick up objects crudely and put them down with a careless bump, we assume that we will be able when the need arises to adapt to the difference between a baby and a bag of groceries. And yet habits carry over and it may be that we do not muster deftness to the extent we are capable, that in fact we have slid our hands under the baby with unintended roughness.

This lack of refinement, unintentional though it may be, can be looked at as an instance of sloth. As the sin of deficient love, sloth is healed halfway up Dante's Mount of Purgatory, above the sins of perverted love (pride, envy, anger) and below the sins of excessive love (avarice, gluttony, and lust). Here in the middle is the sailor's dreaded flat calm, the "noonday demon," "midway between gravity and grace, as if a spaceship had flown beyond the power of attraction of its planet of departure, but could not yet feel the pull of its goal" (Heyneman 1985, 146). Within its dullness our actions become blunted and lose their luster. We get up, dress, fix breakfast and go to work, but at low ebb; we neither refuse the doing nor quite enter into it. Sloth in this broad sense, as a dampening of aliveness, is a deep and pervasive affliction. We find ourselves burdened by its presence and disheartened by its grip on us.

Sloth may crop up in our inclination as a lack of caring. Indifference while driving on the freeway, simply not being interested in the details of maneuvering through traffic, may so tug on normally competent actions that they become dangerous. Or sloth may arise as lack of clarity in perception and execution: though Lisa wishes earnestly to play her bassoon well, her unfocussed hearing of the sounds, coupled with a blurred kinesthetic sense in her fingers, results in tones which are chaotically uncentered and irregular, lacking vibrancy and clear purpose; they do not manifest the loving attention she imagines she gives to her playing.

Slothful action is by its nature often unnoticed. Wendy, coming late into the history class discussion, dragged a chair across the floor, clunked it into place and plopped herself onto it to join the group around the table. The other students first raised their voices to overcome the disturbance and then halted completely until Wendy was settled. This drama occurred beneath the conscious recognition of most of them. Wendy's carelessness contained a measure of almost intentional up-staging; but she was a concerned and conscientious student in most respects, and seen in another light this moment was merely unwitting—an example of the slothfulness which, scarcely regarded, makes its way into our days.

Deftness and Percipience

Recognition can put sloth to rout. Thomas used two simple experiments to demonstrate how sensory awareness can encourage deftness. He had the students sit at a desk and pick up—one after another in their customary manner—the small objects on its surface: a paperclip, a jar of rubber cement, an eraser, pencil, pen, envelope. Then he asked them to pick up a pencil so that all five fingertips came to rest on it at the same instant, with no prior jostling of the pencil—just a clean and immediate grasp-lift.

After they practiced for awhile, they would return to their customary casual picking up of one object after another and observe the action closely, noticing how the hand sometimes dropped afield of the intended object. Perhaps the fingers overshot the mark and had to slide back to form around it; perhaps an unwanted object met them as well, or they jarred needlessly against the desktop. One student commented wryly that he used his hand as if it were an industrial crane scooping up sand in order to sift out the one or two intended bricks.

Thomas would ask them to go back once again to an attentive picking up of the pencil and to notice that as the five fingertips alighted and grasped in unison there seemed to be an ignition of sensory intelligence at their surface. The tips touched and supported the body of the pencil with spritely delicacy.

He also brought to their notice the way that fingers and thumb rested on either side of the pencil like the feet of a bridge while the palm formed an activated span between the contacts. When with their other hand the students felt the front and back of the palm lifting the pencil, they observed active muscular engagement in both the flexors on the palm side and the extensors on the back side. Thomas referred to this integrated state as "core support of the hand." By comparison, when they palpated the grasping hand as it casually picked up objects around the desk they would notice a floppier, less toned quality in the musculature, as if the fingers and thumb were partly disengaged from their embedding in the palm and were thereby less connected to one another. As a final phase of the experiment, Thomas had his students pick up a variety of objects of different sizes and shapes, each as deftly as they had the pencil.

The second experiment in deftness involved saying the word "nimble." Thomas asked students as they repeated the word a few times to notice its sound and then the movement of breath, tongue and lips. For many the sound was muffled by lazy articulating movements. The consonants formed awkwardly around the vowel "i," which was superseded by "m" before it had quite gained its existence.

"Nimble." As they said it, he asked them to notice exactly where the tongue met the hard palate for "n," and to follow the sensation as the articulation traveled toward the back of the mouth to pick up the "i" and then rushed forward to meet the lips on "m," explode outward on "b," and subside as the tongue met the hard palate more flatly on "l."

He suggested that they recollect the qualities of action when they were picking up the pencil with precision—the five fingers at once around the supporting tonus in the palm—and then say "nimble" again, letting the consonants form dextrously around a deliberately more sustained and brighter "i." As they articulated the word they noticed that the entire palate and tongue became more engaged in the speaking, more activated, more spanned between the points of contact that formed the consonants.

Kevin drew a laugh from the class when he called this

"core support of the mouth," but the sound of "nimble" when he spoke it deftly pleased him. Far from having a stagey enunciation, it sprang to life, its meaning more truly reflected in sound. He was training as a high school teacher and was concerned with the sloppiness of his speaking habits. He had thought of taking a public speaking class but had put it off on a hunch that if he simply acquired techniques of elocution his speech would become posed, given to the excessive articulation he found objectionable in some newscasters. Out of the experiment with "nimble" he decided he could improve his speaking on his own, practicing deftness off and on as his manner of speaking entered the field of his attention.

Deftness and Core Support

We can go far in clearing the cobwebs of slothful habits just by noticing the hand as it picks up a telephone receiver or the tongue as it enunciates words. But deftness also depends on the threads which connect the border-detail of our doings with our organic singleness, because actions take place through hierarchical levels of structural differentiation—finger, hand, arm, shoulder girdle. The refinements of the periphery are a foreground expression of deeper levels, just as music's fluctuant details of melody, harmony and texture manifest a more inclusive contrapuntal background. In the light of this hierarchical understanding of movement, the attention of a pianist working to improve dexterity will not be trapped at the surface; futile hours will not be spent practicing only the accurate fingering of a fast passage when attention might more profitably shift at times to the flow of movement in the arms, shoulders and spine, where the upward and downward sweeps of melodic direction are rendered in the larger movements that embrace individual finger-strokes.

Balance, core support and weight release free the connection between periphery and depth, allowing the strength of the pelvic and spinal musculature to express itself in the action of the hands so that the more delicate and refined muscles there are freed from overexertion. The reverberative adjustment of part with part through an adaptable, ever–responsive core of the body puts the whole structure into the service of each of its actions. Span allows the tissue to engage fully in these interconnections. Actions themselves evoke span.

A bridge crossing a river depends upon its two extremities placed on the shore-lip of right and left river banks. In the grasp-lift of a glass, the body reaches between the extremities of the feet on the floor and the fingers on the glass. The action originates simultaneously in feet and fingers. Between them, the body forms the bridge across which the weight-shifts of the reaching movement are directed and released in waves which vibrate to the points of outer contact, floor and glass. Spanned actions are consummated in deft contacts.

Lisa and the rest of the movement class had been exploring core support for several weeks before Thomas led them through the experiments with deftness in hand and tongue. Lisa was struck by a thought: a careful study of how deftness flows from core support might give her dramatic improvement in the two realms she most cared about: bassoon playing and carpentry. She decided to commit herself to a three-month experiment.

That evening Lisa went to a recital by an elderly grand master of piano. She was enthralled by the extraordinary deftness of his fingertips meeting each key, a controlled entry which sounded through acrobatic fast passages and slow lyric passages as a chiselled quality of tone. Yet his body, with spine almost immobile, seemed to be braced stoically against the play of these fingers. At what cost was that dexterity of fingertips wrung from such an uncooperative supporting structure, she pondered, and at what cost to the sound that might have been? The music he created was pleasing and distinctive; but she wondered what would emerge were he to come to better balance, to throw his weight into the phrases from a responsive and flexible spine and to span his contact between fingertips, sitting bones and feet. Without losing its shapely correctness, the sound would be more penetrating, she imagined, would carry more weight of self, with his wryness and elegant aloofness remaining as dimensions folded under. The gains in depth of sound, in forthrightness of passion, were promising.

These observations strengthened her resolve to let a solid and flexible core support undergird her work with the bassoon, though most of her difficulties were directly related to fingers and mouth. When she listened carefully to a tape recording of her playing, she came into focus on three problems: wrong notes, unintended shifts in volume, and faulty rhythm—notes played a little too early or too late to render her precise idea of the music.

Lisa next made a close-up videotape of her fingers playing the bassoon. She was surprised by the clutter of small extraneous jerks and wiggles and by her haphazard placing of fingers on keys or over holes, almost overshooting the mark and then adjusting into place. Sometimes the press and release of keys appeared sluggish. Often fingers that were not in use stuck straight out rigidly and then were unable to move quickly enough when needed. That this chaos of particulars was visible and that she had been oblivious to it while playing was instructive: when she thought she was concentrating, a considerable haze veiled her perception.

As she practiced, Lisa gave her attention first to her balance on the chair and to finding the easiest way of supporting herself and her bassoon. Shifting focus then to the details of finger placement, she realized that core support, by inducing a more peaceful state of mind—particularly because of a release of shoulder and arm tension—had made her fingers more sensitive, more present to her awareness. The haze had cleared somewhat. She was, strangely enough, both more feelingful—more "in" her fingers, more subjective—and at the same time better able to take the kind of objective stance she had had watching the video. Just the double perspective an artist needs, she thought.

As Lisa continued her research for the next few weeks, perfecting the process of moving her awareness between core support, hand action and mouth action, it became increasingly clear that she was improving not only her playing but her way of learning to play. Improved deftness depended on improved quality of attention to detail—that is, on her ability to focus awareness with refinement; and this more effective state of consciousness was, in turn, made possible by the quieter state of mind associated with core support.

The issues were precisely the same when she turned to carpentry. Though Jim, an old, experienced carpenter, the best she had ever worked with, was puzzled and amused when she asked if she could simply watch him for a couple of hours, he saw the value of dedicated close observation once she had explained her purpose to him. Jim's easy elegance in measuring, cutting and hammering was, it seemed to Lisa, the result not just of countless repetitions but of a capacity to move his attention from one fine detail to another with such agility that often you might call it unconscious. She had seen plenty of carpenters as experienced as Jim whose work had continued to be crude because they were not aware at a level of refinement that had become second nature to him.

Unlike the master pianist she had watched, this master carpenter worked with accomplished core support. Watching his hands and fingers closely, she saw that he also demon-strated what Thomas had called core support of the hand, a live, toned connection of fingers into active arches of the palm. Jim's grasp of a hammer as he countersank finishing nails, for instance, was different from her own. Where she held on as if the hammer were a hardened extension of her arm, her fingers simply solidifying the connection, his hand managed to hold firmly and at the same time retain the po-tential for interaction between fingers, so that he struck with more finesse: he had not cut off that last level in the hierarchi-cal differentiation of his structure. It was the secure strength of his balanced torso that allowed his hand to remain so flex-ible and adaptive.

Lisa began observing her carpentry closely—not inces-santly, but off and on. Her study of Jim had been helpful: knowing that there was such a level of refinement, knowing what it looked like in Jim's hand, her imagination was able to guide her, step by step, beyond the sloppiness that had char-acterized her own handlings.

At the end of her three-month experiment Lisa had made gratifying improvements in both playing and carpentry. She was more accurate, more lithe and delicate in the handling of detail, and at the same time more powerful, whether the issue was delivery of tone or the turn of a screwdriver. Even more important to her was that she had begun an ongoing process of learning; she realized that continued conscious attention to detail could train her neuromuscular potential through an unending series of improvements, not only of specific actions but of her general capacity for deft action.

She recalled a thought that had come to her when she was watching the Olympics: that excellence is persistent car-ing. Deftness, she now added, is persistent caring for detail.

Chapter 13

Touch

In humane affairs . . . there is no such thing as competence without love. . . . The events of the field—which are often of the most subtle and elusive kind—cannot even be discerned unless there is a responding sensitivity in the observer. . . . The world is attractive. It is attractive in its sensual forms. Our knowledge of its forms begins in response (which soon becomes creative), and we cannot respond except with our senses. . . . There is no other path except this ground of attracted care by which the events and forms of the world can reach fruition as mind.

George Dennison, *The Lives of Children*
1969, 275–278

The paradox of infinite sexuality is that by regarding sexuality as an expression of the person and not the body, it becomes fully embodied play. It becomes a drama of touching.

James P. Carse, *Finite and Infinite Games* 1986, 85

The Interplay of Action and Percipience

In one version of the story, God, "all ages sitting lonesome in his golden chair," created the universe in order to have someone to play with, to love and be loved by. But since God is being, existence itself, it was impossible to create any thing that was not God, or to step outside the creation in order to meet it, or even to sit back and watch it as an audience. In the nature of the case, God had to be creation as well as creator. And so, in order for there to be any encounter at all, forgetting was also invented. The world was to be an ironic dance where reality meets itself and discovers with amazement what it already knows.

A human is not, according to this story, essentially a doing creature at all, but a perceiver, an appreciator, a spiritual Midas that renders the things we live with back into consciousness by relishing them. If appreciation is our basic human function, its creative outward appearance as religion, art, science, work and play is an artifact of what Rilke called "transformation," a perceptive cherishing that takes place in the silence of a heart that has allowed itself to be entered and altered.

We have surmised that many people, granted a single wish, would opt for depth; they would like their life to penetrate, to be founded in its reality, not just blown here and there by the breezes of circumstance and psychological programming. Thoreau's experiment at Walden Pond was a pursuit of depth, and one appeal of his work is his passionate demonstration that we can deepen our lives by a "conscious endeavor."

> I wished to live deliberately, to front only the essential facts of life, and see if I could not learn what it had to teach, and not, when I came to die, discover that I had

not lived. I did not wish to live what was not life, living is so dear, nor did I wish to practice resignation, unless it was quite necessary. I wanted to live deep and suck out all the marrow of life. . . . (*Walden* [1854] 1962, 172)

Thoreau's strategy was to develop his appreciation of the place he lived in. He honed his alertness, and he organized his activity so that it did not diminish either the inflow of impressions or his capacity to enjoy them. His neighbors thought him lazy.

No one can touch without also being touched. The violinist's finger presses the string—or does the string press the finger? Can one happen without the other? Unless the finger can yield to the impression, it cannot know its own act. The musculoskeletal engine that delivers action also channels perception, and the two directions of energy that flow through it depend on one another.

In lovemaking, where touch is central, the friction of flesh against flesh is only a door, opened by the capacity to both act and feel at the same time. The more deeply the body is allowed to participate by tenderly reverberating its own movements through every fiber and delivering that plenitude to the points of contact, the more bounteously it senses the activity of the other. To give and to receive are inseparable.

Of all our sensory windows on the world, touch is perhaps the one where the outgoing energy of action can most easily overpower the inflow of impressions. Self-confirmation, where personality is asserted as settled attitude or posture, saps sexual engagement of spontaneous sensuality by confining movement to the outer, most voluntary layers of the musculature. Held emotional tension (Reich's armor) sits in the doorway of the encounter, blocking sensation of what is actually happening. Someone who touches another not primarily to feel the touch itself but to stake a claim, send a signal, manipulate a response or pretend a response, acts to that extent from the surface. Acculturation has commonly overcharged us at this operational and calculative end of our neurological spectrum so that such behavior often passes un-noticed—except that sexual engagement, though attractive as fantasy, is often unsatisfying as actual experience. A con-tinual search for new partners or piquant procedures may indicate—and will probably only strengthen—an emphasis on action at the expense of feeling. But the same imbalance may be true of couples who have lived together, "faithfully," for a long time with a predictable and boring sexual ritual, where past clashes of self-confirmation and the resultant guilts, frustrations, disappointments and compromises have driven them into a corner where they can no longer feel one another. It seems to be in the amorous part of life, where we are most strongly motivated toward a free play of impulse and expression, that we are particularly deprived in our capa-city to touch.

To speak of our love play as if it were something to be examined critically and shaped with deliberate intent, raises with poignancy an issue that haunts all of movement learn-ing. We want finally to be rid of ourselves, to enter into our activity spontaneously, innocently, with bodies that are straightforward expressions of consciousness, attention focused outward: the painter absorbed in paint, the scholar in thought, the woodcutter in chopping, the lover in loving, entirely mobilized, without self-consciousness or self-in-dulgence. Generously. A finger that points to the moon and is interested in the moon, not in itself.

The Education of Touch

Emily and Jim had begun to study movement in their mid-thirties as part of a long-standing collaboration to bring life into focus: to clarify values and then shape behavior so that it would manifest their best intentions. The observation and reshaping of movement gave practical goals and procedures which at the same time addressed basic issues, and they threw themselves into this study with enthusiasm.

Over a period of about two years they patiently built up kinesthetic awareness. One issue after another arose as the central focus and then shifted into the background as more inclusive issues emerged: first balance and core support, then weight release, then articulate phrasing. For the past two or three months reverberation had been a major preoccupation; like phrasing it presented issues of sensitivity and response that were larger than the mechanics of movement itself.

Hoeing in the garden one day, Emily was giving attention to reverberation, adjusting core support so that the strength of her legs and pelvis powered the swing of the hoe. As she focused on the release of weight—particularly arms and head—into the momentum of the swing, she felt spinal expansion and allowed the impact of hoe against earth to wash back through all the joints, timing the sequence of swings so that each could fulfill itself and come to rest before the next began.

The sense of connection, person to task, gave her a glow of pleasure. The actual contact was of her hands on the hoe and her feet on the ground, but the balance and release of movement softened the boundaries between herself and the environment and made hoe and dirt seem more a part of her, or herself a part of them. The deliberate organizing of movement fell into the background; adjustments became less-than-conscious means for maintaining an open contact with things and events. It was apparent that the central movement issue was shifting from reverberation to touch. Up until now, finding effective action had also, as a side effect, enhanced her sensitivity to what she touched. Now the process had reversed itself: the enjoyment of a tactile connection with things evoked integrated movement.

A few days later she and Jim watched a television documentary which surveyed research on the importance of touch to humans and other animals (Nova, "A Touch of Sensitivity" 1980). The film showed that people who received even a casual, brushing contact from others become more cheerful and giving. Consistent exposure to affectionate touch is healing to emotionally disturbed children. Monkey babies become psychotic if they are able to see and hear their mothers but cannot touch them. Heart attack patients have a better chance of recovery if they own a dog or a cat, because their heart rate is slowed as they stroke a pet. The program was impressive to Jim and Emily: touching, being touched, is a basic need. Its absence is disintegrative.

Jim and Emily decided that an investigation of touch would be their next developmental adventure. They would begin with ordinary things that they used constantly: toothbrush, fork, chair, steering wheel—objects which, if they were noticed at all, were vaguely regarded as mere utensils. But close attention to contact with all these things was too demanding; to experience just a few fragments of the tactile stimuli of a given moment—the angles on a pencil's shaft against fingers, the grainy texture of the paper, tufts of rug against a bare foot—was enough to overwhelm larger intentions. Letters would not be written nor dinners cooked if all the surfaces touched were brought to active notice. So they

simplified: each chose three or four objects, with the understanding that as occasion arose, one or another of these particular surfaces would receive a moment of undivided awareness. When they had repeatedly and thoroughly appreciated
them, other objects would be chosen for tactile study.

Emily's discovery while hoeing was borne out repeatedly: to heed touch improves an action. One of Jim's projects
was to be aware of tactile feedback from the tennis racquet.
As with nearly every activity examined, the first and most
obvious result was a reduction in tension. His whole body,
responding to the softened grip, suited its level of effort more
accurately to the demands of the game; he dropped into core
support and released arm and head weight to swing with
freer momentum into action. Shots were stronger and truer.
His anxiety level fell as he released this non-functional overlay of muscular contraction, and he experienced a strange
sense that he had more time to maneuver, though his opponent said his game was moving faster. Emily found that she
could often parallel park in one try if she paid careful attention to the play of the steering wheel in her hands. When she
concentrated on this she was less flustered, less defeated by
past parking embarrassments and better aware of the total
situation.

With quietness also came pleasure in actions taken and
in living among things. The decision to touch was an implicit
intention to enjoy, and they did. In their spiritual explorations they had learned to value above all a shift of perspective
that brought a more real, and ultimately a friendlier, contact
with their present world. Religious literature did not always
teach what they now experienced. To refine and enjoy the
sense of touch was not, as some traditions assumed, an in-
dulgence that encouraged compulsive attachment to "the
world," but quite to the contrary was an easing of participa-

tion in the environment; they were less anxious and more loving in their moment-by-moment existence and were glad to find a practical way to lift the quality of the mundane—to find a spiritual discipline in washing the dishes. Awareness of movement had cut a trail that mindful touch now extended; a focus outward into "the events and forms of the world" helped them in becoming more innocently the instrument of action, with less sentimentality, cynicism or boredom.

Emily, who wished above all not to brush by the world in a whirl of busyness, experimented with the expression of care through touch. She slowed down when she picked vegetables in the garden and she allowed the sensations to resonate, closing her eyes sometimes and taking time to feel the bumps on a cucumber, the springy texture of its flesh, the snap of the stem as she broke it off. Such a cucumber was different—not just as her teeth, tongue and throat touched it with feeling, but in the quality of what could be called gratitude, which became less theoretical. She found that she often went barefoot around the house, and enjoyed the contrasts of texture and temperature from carpet to wood to tiles. For a few weeks the feel of different fabrics against her skin was a fascination; another tack carried her into the amazing profusion of contours—knobs, spoons, fence posts—that had been around her all the time, their beauty mostly unrecognized in her tactile blindness.

Trapped in muffled, hurried guitar playing, Emily explored touch as an aesthetic guide. Jim had drawn her attention to the way she played a passage over and over without any apparent change, as if sheer repetition would somehow win musicianship. When she paid careful heed to the guitar strings against her fingers, the first thing she noticed was that the contact hurt. Her fingertips tightened against the pain, and then tension blocked sensory input. Could the pressure of her fingers be lighter without a loss of tone or of pitch control? She discovered that her left wrist, cocked back to put the hand into position, was also rigid, and that she sat in a contracted flexion, wrapped around the instrument. Improved balance unwrapped her torso, the sensation of arm weight invited her shoulders to relax and her wrist to open; she could then press the strings in a way that did not hurt and that centered the tone and aided finger accuracy. To change her touch on the strings involved this whole sentient background. A line from a Thomas Hardy novel, which described a character as "so ethereal a creature that her spirit could be seen trembling through her limbs" became (not without an ironic smile at the extravagance of the image) an inspirational node for plucking the guitar (*Jude the Obscure* [1895] 1980, 187).

When Emily brought the two sensory modes together—heard what fingers felt, felt through fingers what she heard—both tactile and aural senses were heightened and she began to phrase practice sessions differently. A pause after playing a passage allowed both touch and sound to resonate to stillness, so that when she repeated the passage she had a specific intention that arose from sensory experience. Jim commented that repetitions were leading her through progressive changes rather than grinding a groove deeper and deeper.

It seemed to Emily as though the pain in her fingers had been relieved not just by a change in the contact but by mindfulness itself, and this intuition led to a new realm of exploration. She had once heard pain defined as "the impulse to withdraw"; this fascinated her now, because it implied that pain is not a sensation but a reaction to sensation. When her reaction to the pressure of strings against fingers changed from unconscious withdrawal to active scrutiny, what she felt was no longer experienced as pain.

One day in the garden, when she twisted her ankle, she

inhibited a first impulse to hop around on the other foot, moaning and complaining; instead she became quiet, relaxed her muscles, and focused directly on what she was experiencing. It remained what it was, an intense sensation, but it was not pain. The same thing happened in the dentist's chair when she had a tooth repaired without anesthetic: so long as she maintained focus (which sometimes took all her power of concentration) and did not tighten or pull away, she experienced strongly, but did not experience pain.

Jim took some lessons from Samantha, their finicky, high-strung, affectionate Irish setter. He began to notice that her enjoyment of his petting was sometimes mixed with slight cringes, and that he often came at her with an overcharge of nervous energy. He hurt her as he vigorously thumped her sides or scratched behind her ears—or he made her afraid of being hurt. To feel the texture of her fur and the loose skin under it, to mold the contours of flesh and bone with his entire hand—to appreciate her in sensuous detail (which at the same time expressed that appreciation) became a gratifying experience to both.

To touch one another with sensitive awareness was a complex undertaking for Jim and Emily; their contact often reflected a charged psychological program, and scrutiny revealed motives that were unpleasant or embarrassing to uncover. A dimension of Jim's touch was imperialistic. When he placed an ostensibly affectionate arm around Emily's shoulder or grasped her waist from behind, he at times was delivering a thinly disguised expression of control, often a prelude to demands veiled as requests or suggestions. To weed out this slyly aggressive behavior Jim decided not to cut off the gestures but to complete them with awareness on their tactile sensation; they needed transformation, not suppression. Gradually he learned to recognize the hard edge of muscular contraction that embodied this false front. He could find, behind his own held "position" vis-à-vis Emily, a more mobile and responsive gesture.

He began to realize that his touch, which might have offered connection, had been twisted by unwitting acculturation into a manipulative tool which separated him from others. Outside the family an intimate touch was often not a viable option: social convention had so strongly associated touch with sexual meanings that Jim was afraid that feelingful contact, except in well-defined rituals such as a handshake, would be understood as a "come-on." He himself felt this strong association of touch with sex; it lay behind his shyness in touching others, as he recognized one evening in a theater lobby. Threading his way through the crowd, he noticed that he shrank from the light, brushing contacts that were, under the circumstances, almost unavoidable. It was a relief to enjoy them as transient sensory experiences and to let their overtones melt away.

Lovemaking was abundantly expressive in this close-knit marriage, but old patterns of resentment and frustration sometimes isolated the two as they sought for one another in a mutually spontaneous flow of playful movement. Tactile awareness—simple, immediate and pleasurable—served them well.

Spiritual, Aesthetic, and Ecological Dimensions of Generous Movement

Movement learning can find higher ground in the exploration of touch. The journey into one's own structure, now turning outward, evolves into appreciation of the surroundings. This evolution is implicit in the basic principle that we have named "generous movement": the balance, release and support of one's weight are a rediscovery of how we are designed to live within the force field of gravitational energy; reverberation, an expression of individual wholeness, is at the same time the measure of one's capacity for sensitive interaction; phrasing can be graceful and effective only by adaptation to surrounding rhythms. This cluster of inter-twined disciplines leads to a quiet and receptive state of con-sciousness, one able to receive and integrate the flowing forms of the world through touch and other sensory modes. The growth of percipience—both the inwardness of sensory self-knowledge and the outwardness that is its natural ac-companiment (what we have called "stalking") turns life from self-aggrandizement to celebration. The things around us speak clearly, with their own voice, because we are able to listen with care.

The value of a shift in one's style of consciousness, to-ward peaceful alertness, though often honored in the breach, is hardly to be questioned. Religions that teach love as the raison d'être of existence assume that genuine loyalty to awakened insight will be learned, and expressed, in loving behavior. If the very fiber of activity—the pattern of motion and self-support that executes action—is itself an expression of value and attitude, underlying and partially determining intentions, then systematic transformation of movement is an important arena for anyone on a path of spiritual growth. Prayer, meditation, and acts of loving kindness carried out in a posture of defensive anxiety will to some extent be contra-dicted by their very medium of expression.

And if the natural, undistorted human form, evolved through countless billions of interactions with earth's gravita-tional field, is designed for a more open, joyful, giving and accepting flow with the environment than our culture has taught us, then a discipline of sustained change in the movement habits of our most ordinary doings can guide us toward genuine and fully realized expressiveness. Touch, as an instance of loving behavior, became the focus of movement study for Emily and Jim because of their spiritual concern; it gave them a specific, repeatable method of progressive self-discovery and put the awareness of movement into the context that most interested them.

For others, represented frequently in the narrative parts of this book, an aesthetic focus is central: where the shapeliness and "speaking" quality of movement are projected by means of musical instruments; or where the body is its own instrument—in dance, acting, singing and speech; or where tools such as brushes or chisels are applied to materials which retain, as paintings or sculptures, the expressive quality of the movements that produced them. The aesthetic impulse will also be dominant where grace and flair in daily life have become important to an individual. Because movement and posture are expressive, life is inevitably an artistic venture that we choreograph as we go along.

To be sure, the distinction between "aesthetic" and "spiritual" is hazy. In the practice of their craft, artists are likely to concentrate on the surface levels of expression, the refinement of peripheral detail, while spiritually-directed people are more likely to be interested in the deeper background where, as a Zen koan puts it, "form is formlessness and formlessness is form." Just as an artwork depends on a rendered depth for its integrity, and the carrying-out of spiritual discipline in myriad details of life gives religion its actuality, so developing one's movement can become inspiring when it merges the artistic and spiritual levels:

> "Beauty is truth, truth beauty,"—that is all
> Ye know on earth and all ye need to know. (Keats, *Ode on a Grecian Urn*)

Keats is showing us a playful, potentially a joyful, perspective from which to enact one's life, a healthy antidote to both the deadening seriousness and the triviality of an exploitive culture.

Sometimes the consequences of weaving bonds of love with the world and of searching into one's own depths is suffering. Growth toward a generous movement style is therefore paradoxical: the release of large and small habits of neurotic recoil, which have continually cycled us back into misery, will obviously leave us in a happier and healthier state; but since many of these habits were acquired in order to avoid pain, working through them means facing up to what has been sidestepped in the past. Rilke called sorrow "our winter-enduring foliage, our dark green of meaning," and pictured human joy as a stream that flowed from the mountains of primeval sorrow (*The Tenth Duino Elegy* [1923] 1989). The central Christian symbol is the cross. The falling tears of the pre-Inca universal father-god Viracocha are drops of rain falling to the earth: sorrow is the source of life itself.

Reshaping movement is a call to the courage of sentience.

Bibliography

Aguado, Oscar, in collaboration with David Zucker. *The Form*. Laguna Beach, CA: School of the Form, 1978.

Aguado, Oscar. *Gravity: The Nether Side of Paradise*. Laguna Beach, CA: School of the Form, 1978.

Alexander, F. Matthias. *Constructive Conscious Control of the Individual*. Downey, CA: Centerline Press, 1985. (Originally published 1923.)

Alexander, F. Matthias. *Man's Supreme Inheritance: Conscious Guidance and Control in Relation to Human Evolution in Civilization*. London: Methuen, 1918.

*Alexander, F. Matthias. *The Resurrection of the Body*. Selected and introduced by Edward Maisel. New York: Dell, 1969.

Alexander, F. Matthias. *The Universal Constant in Living*. Manchester: Re-education Publications, 1947. (Originally published 1941.)

Particularly relevant materials are preceded by an asterisk.

Alexander, F. Matthias. *The Use of the Self.* Downey, CA: Centerline Press, 1984. (Originally published 1932.)

Alexander, Gerda. *Eutony: The Holistic Discovery of the Total Person.* Great Neck, NY: Felix Morrow, 1985.

Allport, Gordon W., and Philip E. Vernon. *Studies in Expressive Movement.* New York: Macmillan, 1933.

Arnheim, Daniel. *Dance Injuries: Their Prevention and Care.* St. Louis: Mosby, 1980.

Bailey, Covert. *Fit or Fat?* Boston: Houghton Mifflin, 1978.

de Balzac, Honoré. *Père Goriot.* Translated by E. K. Brown. New York: Modern Library, 1950. (Original French publication 1834.)

Barker, Sarah. *The Alexander Technique: The Revolutionary Way to Use Your Body for Total Energy.* New York: Bantam, 1978.

Barlin, Anne Lief, and Tamara Greenberg. *Move and Be Moved: A Practical Approach to Movement with Meaning.* Los Angeles: Learning Through Movement, 1980.

*Barlow, Wilfred. *The Alexander Technique.* New York: Knopf, 1977.

*Bartenieff, Irmgard, with Dori Lewis. *Body Movement: Coping with the Environment.* New York: Gordon and Breach, 1980.

Bates, William. *The Cure of Imperfect Eyesight by Treatment without Glasses.* New York: Central Fixation Publishing Co., 1920.

Berger, Arthur. "New Linguistic Modes and the New Theory." *Perspectives of New Music* 3, No. 1: 1–9.

Berry, Cicely. *Voice and the Actor.* New York: Macmillan, 1974.

*Bertherat, Thérèse, and Carol Bernstein. *The Body Has Its Reasons: Anti-Exercises and Self-Awareness.* New York: Pantheon, 1977.

Boethius. *The Consolation of Philosophy.* Translated by Richard Green. Indianapolis: Bobbs, Merrill, 1962. (Originally written 524.)

Bonpensiere, Luigi. *New Pathways to Piano Technique: A Study of the Relations between Mind and Body with Special Reference to Piano Playing*. New York: Philosophical Library, 1953.

Boone, J. Allen. *Kinship with All Life*. New York: Harper & Row, 1954.

Brecht, Bertolt. "A Short Organum for the Theater." In *Brecht on Theatre: The Development of an Aesthetic*, edited and translated by John Willett. New York: Hill & Wang, 1964. (Original German publication 1947–1948.)

*Brooks, Charles V. W. *Sensory Awareness: The Rediscovery of Experiencing*. Santa Barbara: Ross-Erickson, 1978.

Brunnstrom, Signe. *Clinical Kinesiology*. Philadelphia: Davis, 1972.

Buber, Martin. *I and Thou*. Translated by Ronald Smith. New York: Scribners, 1958.

Buber, Martin. *Tales of the Hasidim*. 2 volumes. New York: Schocken, 1947.

Cage, John. *Silence: Lectures and Writings*. Middletown, CT: Wesleyan University Press, 1961.

Cailliet, Rene. *Low Back Pain Syndrome*. Second Edition. Philadelphia: Davis, 1968.

Cailliet, Rene. *Foot and Ankle Pain*. Philadelphia: Davis, 1968.

Cailliet, Rene. *Hand Pain and Impairment*. Philadelphia: Davis, 1971.

Cailliet, Rene. *Knee Pain and Disability*. Philadelphia: Davis, 1973.

Cailliet, Rene. *Neck and Arm Pain*. Philadelphia: Davis, 1964.

Cailliet, Rene. *Scoliosis: Diagnosis and Management*. Philadelphia: Davis, 1975.

Cailliet, Rene. *Shoulder Pain*. Philadelphia: Davis, 1966.

*Cailliet, Rene. *Soft Tissue Pain and Disability*. Philadelphia: Davis, 1977.

Campbell, Joseph. *The Hero with a Thousand Faces*. Cleveland: World, 1956.

Cannon, Walter. *The Wisdom of the Body*. New York: Norton, 1963. (Originally published 1932.)

Capra, Fritjof. *The Tao of Physics: An Exploration of the Parallels* between *Modern Physics and Eastern Mysticism*. Boulder: Shambhala, 1975.

Carlsöö, Sven. *How Man Moves: Kinesiological Methods and Studies*. London: Heineman, 1972.

Carse, James P. *Finite and Infinite Games: A Vision of Life as Play and Possibility*. New York: Free Press, 1986.

Carse, James P. *The Silence of God*. New York: Macmillan, 1985.

Castaneda, Carlos. *A Separate Reality*. New York: Pocket Books, 1983.

Chase, Mildred. *Just Being at the Piano*. Culver City, CA: Peace Press, 1981.

Chekhov, Michael. *To the Actor: On the Technique of Acting*. New York: Harper & Row, 1953.

Clines, Manfred. *Sentics: The Touch of Emotions*. Garden City: Anchor, 1978.

Cogan, Robert, and Pozzi Escot. *Sonic Design: The Nature of Sound and Music*. Englewood Cliffs, NJ: Prentice-Hall, 1976.

Coleridge, Samuel Taylor. *Biographia Literaria*. Edited with his Aesthetical Essays by John Shawcross. Two volumes. London: Oxford University, 1907. (Originally published 1917.)

Cone, Edward. *Musical Form and Musical Performance*. New York: Norton, 1968.

Conrad, Joseph. *The Portable Conrad*. Edited by Morten Dawen Zabel. New York: Penguin, 1976.

Cousins, Norman. *Anatomy of an Illness as Perceived by the Patient: Reflections on Healing and Regeneration*. New York: Bantam, 1981.

Cousins, Norman. *The Healing Heart: Antidotes to Panic and Helplessness*. New York: Norton, 1983.

cummings, e. e. *Poems: 1923–1954*. New York: Harcourt, Brace, 1954.

Da Free John. *The Bodily Location of Happiness*. Clearlake, CA: Dawn Horse, 1982.

*Dart, Raymond A. "Voluntary Musculature in the Human

Body: The Double-Spiral Arrangement." *British Journal of Physical Medicine* 13 (1950): 265–268.

Darwin, Charles. *The Expression of the Emotions in Man and Animals*. Chicago: University of Chicago, 1965.

Dawkins, Richard. *The Selfish Gene*. New York: Oxford University Press, 1976.

Dennison, George. *The Lives of Children: The Story of the First Street School*. New York: Random House, 1969.

Dennison, George. *Luisa Domic*. New York: Harper & Row, 1985.

*Doczi, György. *The Power of Limits: Proportional Harmonies in Nature, Art and Architecture*. Boulder: Shambhala, 1981.

Dossey, Larry. *Beyond Illness: Discovering the Experience of Health*. Boston: Shambhala, 1984.

*Dossey, Larry. *Space, Time and Medicine*. Boulder: Shambhala, 1982.

Downing, George. *The Massage Book*. New York: Random House, 1972.

Duerckheim, Karlfried. *Hara: The Vital Centre of Man*. New York: Weiser, 1962.

Duerckheim, Karlfried. *The Way of Transformation: Daily Life as Spiritual Exercise*. London: George Allen and Unwin, 1985. (Originally published 1962.)

Dychtwald, Ken. *Bodymind*. Los Angeles: Tarcher, 1986.

Eckhart, Meister. *Meister Eckhart: A Modern Translation*. Translated by Raymond Blakney. New York: Harper & Brothers, 1941. (Originally written 14th century.)

Ehrenzweig, Anton. *The Hidden Order of Art*. Berkeley: University of California, 1971.

Eliot, T. S. *The Complete Poems and Plays*. New York: Harcourt, Brace, 1952.

Ellenberger, W., H. Dittrich, and H. Baum. *An Atlas of Animal Anatomy for Artists*. Edited by Lewis S. Brown. New York: Dover, 1949.

Essene Gospel of Peace. Quotation cited in *How to Grow More Vegetables: A Primer on the Life-Giving Biodynamic/French*

Intensive Method of Organic Horticulture by John Jeavons. Berkeley: Ten Speed, 1979, i.

Farquhar, John. *The American Way of Life Need Not Be Hazardous to Your Health*. New York: Norton, 1978.

*Feitis, Rosemary, editor. *Ida Rolf Talks About Rolfing and Physical Reality*. New York: Harper & Row, 1978.

Feldenkrais, M. *Awareness through Movement: Health Exercises for Personal Growth*. New York: Harper & Row, 1972.

*Feldenkrais, M. *Body and Mature Behavior: A Study of Anxiety, Sex, Gravitation and Learning*. New York: International Universities Press, 1949.

Feldenkrais, M. *The Case of Nora: Body Awareness as Healing Therapy*. New York: Harper & Row, 1977.

Feldenkrais, M. *The Elusive Obvious*. Cupertino, CA: Meta, 1981.

*Fenton, Jack. *Practical Movement Control*. Boston: Plays, Inc., 1973.

Ferguson, Donald. *Music as Metaphor: The Elements of Expression*. Westport, CT: Greenwood, 1973.

Findlay, Elsa. *Rhythm and Movement: Applications of Dalcroze Eurhythmics*. Evanston, IL: Summy-Birchard, 1971.

Forti, Simone. *Handbook in Motion*. Halifax: The Press of the Nova Scotia College of Art and Design, 1974.

Franck, Frederick. *Art as a Way: A Return to the Spiritual Roots*. New York: Crossroad, 1981.

Franck, Frederick. *The Zen of Seeing*. New York: Random House, 1973.

*Friedman, Meyer, and Ray Rosenman. *Type A Behavior and Your Heart*. Greenwich, CT: Fawcett, 1974.

*Fries, James F,. and Lawrence M. Crapo. *Vitality and Aging: Implications of the Rectangular Curve*. San Francisco: W. H. Freeman, 1981.

Fuller, R. Buckminster, and E. J. Applewhite. *Synergetics*. New York: Macmillan, 1975.

Fullerson, Mary C. *By a New and Living Way*. Berkeley: Shambhala, 1974.

*Gallwey, Timothy. *Inner Tennis: Playing the Game*. New York: Random House, 1976.

Gallwey, Timothy, and Bob Kriegel. *Inner Skiing*. New York: Random House, 1977.

*Gendlin, Eugene. *Focusing*. Second edition. New York: Bantam, 1981.

*Golas, Thaddeus. *The Lazy Man's Guide to Enlightenment*. Palo Alto, CA: Seed Center, 1972.

Goodman, Nelson. *Languages of Art*. Indianapolis: Bobbs-Merrill, 1968.

Gorman, David. *The Body Moveable: Blueprints of the Human Musculoskeletal System, Its Structure, Mechanics, Locomotor and Postural Functions*. 3 volumes. Vancouver: David Gorman, 1981.

Guggenbuehl-Craig, Adolf. *Power in the Helping Professions*. Dallas: Spring, 1971.

Hamel, Peter. *Through Music to the Self*. Boulder: Shambhala, 1979.

*Hanna, Thomas. *The Body of Life*. New York: Knopf, 1983.

Hanna, Thomas. *Bodies in Revolt: A Primer of Somatic Thinking*. New York: Holt, Rinehart & Winston, 1970.

Hardy, Thomas. *Far from the Madding Crowd*. New York: Harper, 1918. (Originally published 1897.)

Hardy, Thomas. *Jude the Obscure*. New York: New American Library, 1961. (Originally published 1895.)

Heckler, Richard. *The Anatomy of Change: East-West Approaches to Body-Mind Therapy*. Boulder: Shambhala, 1984.

Heidegger, Martin. *Poetry, Language, Thought*. New York: Harper & Row, 1971.

Heller, Joseph, and William A. Henkin. *Bodywise: Regaining Your Flexibility and Vitality for Maximum Well-being*. Los Angeles: Tarcher, 1986.

Herrigel, Eugen. *Zen in the Art of Archery*. Translated by R. F. C. Hull. New York: Random House, 1971.

Heyneman, Martha. "Sloth." *Parabola* X, no. 4 (1985): 16–18.

Hillesum, Etty. *An Interrupted Life: The Diaries of Etty Hillesum, 1941–43.* New York: Washington Square Press, 1985.

Hofstadter, Douglas. *Gödel, Escher, Bach: An Eternal Golden Braid.* New York: Random House, 1980.

Hollinshead, W. Henry, and David Jenkins. *Functional Anatomy of the Limbs and Back.* Philadelphia: Saunders, 1981.

Hora, Thomas. *Beyond the Dream.* Orange, CA: PAGL Press, 1985.

Hora, Thomas. *Dialogues in Metapsychiatry.* New York: Seabury, 1977.

*Hora, Thomas. *Existential Metapsychiatry.* New York: Seabury, 1977.

Huang, Al Chung-liang. *Embrace Tiger, Return to Mountain: The Essence of T'ai Chi.* Moab, UT: Real People Press, 1973.

Hunt, Valerie. "The Biological Organization of Man to Move." *Impulse* (1968): 51–63.

Hunt, Valerie, W. Massey, R. Weinberg, R. Bruyere, and P. Hahn. *A Study of Structural Integration from Neuromuscular, Energy Field, and Emotional Approaches.* Unpublished Project Report (UCLA), 1977.

Huxley, Aldous. *The Art of Seeing.* Seattle: Montana Books, 1975.

Inman, Verne, Henry Ralston, and Frank Todd. *Human Walking.* Baltimore: Williams and Wilkins, 1981.

Jacobi, Jolande. *The Way of Individuation.* New York: New American Library (Meridian), 1983.

Jacobson, Edmund. *You Must Relax: Practical Methods for Reducing the Tensions of Modern Living.* Fifth edition. New York: McGraw-Hill, 1978.

Johnson, Don. *The Body.* Boston: Beacon, 1983.

Johnson, Don. *The Protean Body.* New York: Harper & Row, 1977.

Johnston, William. *Silent Music: The Science of Meditation.* New York: Harper & Row, 1979.

Jones, Frank Pierce. *Body Awareness in Action: A Study of the Alexander Technique.* New York: Schocken, 1976.

Juhan, Deane. *Job's Body: A Handbook for Bodywork*. Barry-town, NY: Station Hill, 1987.

Jung, Carl G. *Answer to Job*. Translated by R. F. C. Hull. Cleveland: World, 1960.

Jung, Carl G. *Modern Man in Search of a Soul*. Translated by W. S. Dell and Cary F. Baynes. New York: Harcourt, Brace and World, 1966.

Jung, Carl G., M.-L. von Franz, J. Henderson, J. Jacobi, and A. Jaffe. *Man and His Symbols*. New York: Dell, 1968.

Kahle, W., H. Leonhardt, W. Platzer. *Color Atlas and Textbook of Human Anatomy. Volume 1: Locomotor System* (by Werner Platzer). Chicago: Year Book Medical Publishers, 1978.

Kaiser, Hellmuth. *Effective Psychotherapy*. Edited by Louis Fierman. New York: Free Press, 1965.

*Kapandji, I. A. *The Physiology of the Joints*. 3 volumes. Edinburgh: Churchill Livingstone, 1970.

Kapit, Wynn, and Lawrence Elson. *The Anatomy Coloring Book*. New York: Harper & Row, 1977.

Keleman, Stanley. *Emotional Anatomy*. Berkeley, Center Press, 1985.

Kelley, Charles. *New Techniques of Vision Improvement*. Santa Monica, CA: Interscience Work Shop, 1971.

Kendall, Henry, Florence Kendall, and Dorothy Boynton. *Posture and Pain*. Huntington, NY: Krieger, 1970.

Kenneson, Claude. *A Cellist's Guide to the New Approach*. New York: Exposition, 1974.

Keyes, Laurel. *Toning: the Creative Power of the Voice*. Marina del Rey, CA: DeVorss, 1973.

*Kirkby, Ron. "The Probable Reality behind Structural Integration." *Bulletin of Structural Integration* 5 (1975): 5.

Kivy, Peter. *The Corded Shell: Reflections on Musical Expression*. Princeton: Princeton University, 1980.

Kivy, Peter. *Sound and Semblance: Reflections on Musical Representation*. Princeton: Princeton University, 1984.

Kleinman, Seymour, editor. *Mind and Body: East Meets West*. Champaign, IL: Human Kinetics, 1985.

*Kogan, Gerald, editor. *Your Body Works*. Berkeley, Transformations Press, 1980.

Kuebler-Ross, Elizabeth. *On Death and Dying*. New York: Macmillan, 1970.

Kugler, Paul. *The Alchemy of Discourse: An Archetypal Approach to Language*. Lewisburg: Bucknell University, 1982.

Laban, Rudolf. *The Language of Movement: A Guidebook to Choreutics*. Annotated and edited by Lisa Ullman. Boston: Plays, Inc., 1974.

Laban, Rudolf. *The Mastery of Movement*. Third edition. Revised by Lisa Ullman. London: MacDonald and Evans, 1971.

Laban, Rudolf, and F. C. Lawrence. *Effort: Economy in Body Movement*. Second edition. Boston: Plays, Inc., 1974.

Lamb, Warren. *Body Code*. London: Routledge and Kegan Paul, 1979.

*Lee, Jennette. *This Magic Body*. New York: Viking, 1946.

Lenihan, John. *Human Engineering: The Body Re-examined*. New York: Braziller, 1975.

Lessac, Arthur. *Body Wisdom: The Use and Training of the Human Body*. New York: Drama Book Specialists, 1981.

Lessac, Arthur. *The Use and Training of the Human Voice: A Practical Approach to Speech and Voice Dynamics*. New York: Drama Book Specialists, 1967.

Levarie, Siegmund, and Ernst Levy. *Tone: A Study in Musical Acoustics*. Second Edition. Kent, OH: Kent State University Press, 1980.

*Levine, Stephen M. "Continuous Tension, Discontinuous Compression: A Model for Biomechanical Support of the Body." *Bulletin of Structural Integration* 8, No. 1, 1982:31.

Lidov, David. "Mind and Body in Music." *Semiotica* 66–1/3 (1987), 69–97.

*Linklater, Kristin. *Freeing the Natural Voice*. New York: Drama Book Specialists, 1976.

Lovelock, J. E. *Gaia: A New Look at Life on Earth*. London: Oxford University Press, 1979.

Lowen, Alexander. *Bioenergetics*. New York: Penguin, 1976.

Lowen, Alexander. *Pleasure: A Creative Approach to Life*. New York: Penguin, 1975.

MacConaill, M. A., and J. V. Basmajian. *Muscles and Movements: A Basis for Human Kinesiology*. New revised edition. Huntington, NY: Krieger, 1977.

Mangione, Michele. "Movement Enhancement: A Physical-Spiritual-Psychological Approach to Movement Education." Master's thesis, University Without Walls, 1984.

McCluggage, Denise. *The Centered Skier*. Waitsfield, VT: Vermont Crossroads Press, 1977.

Mees, L. F. *Secrets of the Skeleton: Form in Metamorphosis*. Edited by Ellen Bohr and David Adams. Hudson, NY: Anthroposophic Press, 1984.

Merton, Thomas. *A Hidden Wholeness: The Visual World of Thomas Merton*. Text by John Howard Griffin. Photographs by Thomas Merton and John Howard Griffin. New York: Houghton Mifflin, 1979.

Merton, Thomas. *Seven Storey Mountain*. New York: Harcourt, Brace, Jovanovich, 1976.

*Middendorf, Ilse. "The Meaning of Breathing." In *Your Body Works: A Guide to Health, Energy and Balance*, edited by Gerald Kogan. Berkeley: Transformations Press, 1980, 101–114.

Miller, Alice. *For Your Own Good: Hidden Cruelty in Childrearing and the Roots of Violence*. New York: Farrar, Strauss & Giroux, l983.

Minsky, Marvin. *The Society of Mind*. New York: Simon & Schuster, 1986.

Montagu, Ashley. *Touching: The Human Significance of the Skin*. New York: Harper & Row, 1972.

Morris, Desmond. *Manwatching: A Field Guide to Human Behavior*. New York: Abrams, 1977.

Morris, Eric, and Joan Hotchkis. *No Acting Please*. Los Angeles: Whitehouse-Spelling, 1979.

Moss, Donald. "Brain, Body, and World: Perspectives on Body-Image." In *Existential-Phenomenological Alternatives for Psychology*, edited by Ronald Valle and Mark King. New York: Oxford, 1978.

Nillson, Lennart, in collaboration with Jan Lindberg. *Behold Man: A Photographic Journey of Discovery inside the Body*. Boston: Little, Brown, 1974.

Nova. "Animal Olympians." BBC, 1980.

Nova. "A Touch of Sensitivity." BBC, 1980.

Onions, C.T., G. W. S. Friedrichsen, and R. W. Burchfield. *The Oxford Dictionary of English Etymology*. Oxford: Oxford University, 1966.

Ostrander, Sheila, and Lynn Schroeder, with Nancy Ostrander. *Superlearning*. New York: Delacorte Press, 1979.

Pascal, Blaise. *Pensées*. Edited by T. S. Eliot. London: Dent, 1931.

Pelletier, Kenneth. *Mind as Healer, Mind as Slayer: A Holistic Approach to Preventing Stress Disorders*. New York: Dell, 1977.

Perls, Frederick. *Gestalt Therapy Verbatim*. Compiled and edited by John O. Stevens. Lafayette, CA: Real People Press, 1969.

Perls, Frederick. *Hunger, Ego and Aggression: The Beginning of Gestalt Therapy*. New York: Random House, 1969.

*Pernkopf, Eduard. *Atlas of Topographical and Applied Human Anatomy*. 2 volumes. Philadelphia: W. B. Saunders, 1963.

Pesso, Albert. *Movement in Psychotherapy: Psychomotor Techniques and Training*. New York: New York University, 1969.

Pickering, S. G. *Exercises for the Autonomic Nervous System: You Need Them!* Springfield, IL: Thomas, 1981.

Pierce, Alexandra. "Character and Characterization in Musical Performance: Effects of Sensory Experience upon Meaning." Unpublished essay, 1989.

Pierce, Alexandra. "Music and Movement." In *The Semiotic Web '86: An International Yearbook*, edited by Thomas A. Sebeok and Jean Umiker-Sebeok. Berlin: Mouton de Gruyter, 1987.

*Pierce, Alexandra. *Spanning: Essays on Music Theory, Performance, and Movement*. Redlands, CA: Center of Balance, 1982.

*Pierce, Alexandra, and Roger Pierce. "Pain and Healing:For

Pianists." *The Piano Quarterly* 118 (Summer 1982): 43–47; 122 (Summer 1983): 38–40; 126 (Summer 1984): 45–49.

Pierce, Anne A. (Alexandra). "The Analysis of Rhythm in Tonal Music." Unpublished Ph.D. dissertation, Brandeis University, 1968.

*Pierce, Roger. "Doing Bodywork as a Spiritual Discipline." *Somatics* 4, No. 3 (Autumn-Winter 1983–84): 19–26.

Pierce, Roger. "Irony in Schlegel's *Fragments*, Tieck's *Puss in Boots*, and Kleist's *Amphitryon*." *Southern Speech Journal* 35 (1969): 61–70.

Pierce, Roger. "Three Play Analyses." Unpublished Ph.D. dissertation, University of Iowa, 1969.

Pilgrim, Richard B. "Intervals (Ma) in Space and Time: Foundations for a Religio-Aesthetic Paradigm in Japan." *History of Religions*, February (1986).

Prall, D. W. *Aesthetic Analysis*. New York: Thomas Y. Crowell, 1936.

Proust, Marcel. *Remembrance of Things Past*. Three volumes. Translated by C. K. Scott Moncrieff and Terence Kilmartin. New York: Random House, 1981. (Original French publication 1913–1927.)

Ram, Dass and Paul Gorman. *How Can I Help?* New York: Knopf, 1987.

Rasch, Philip, and Roger Burke. *Kinesiology and Applied Anatomy: The Science of Human Movement*. Sixth edition. Philadelphia: Lea and Febiger, 1978.

Reich, Wilhelm. *The Function of the Orgasm*. New York: Noonday, 1942.

Riffaterre, Michael. *Semiotics of Poetry*. Bloomington: Indiana University Press, 1978.

Rilke, Rainer Maria. "The Duino Elegies." Translated by Dora Van Vranken, Alexandra Pierce and Roger Pierce. Unpublished manuscript, 1989.

Rilke, Rainer Maria. "Force of Gravity." Translated by Roger Pierce. Unpublished manuscript, 1987. (The German original appears in *The Selected Poetry of Rainer Maria*

Rilke, edited by Stephen Mitchell. [New York: Vintage, 1984], p. 270.)

Ristad, Eloise. *A Soprano on Her Head.* Moab, UT: Real People Press, 1982.

Roberts, Jane. *The Nature of Personal Reality.* New York: Bantam, 1978.

Roche, Mary Alice. "Elsa Gindler, 1885–1961." Charlotte Selver Foundation *Bulletin* Vol. II, no. 10, (Winter 1981).

Roche, Mary Alice. "Gertrud Falke Heller, 1891–1984." Charlotte Selver Foundation *Newsletter* (Summer 1984): 8.

Rogers, Carl. *On Becoming a Person: A Therapist's View of Psychotherapy.* Boston: Houghton Mifflin, 1970.

*Rolf, Ida P. *Rolfing: The Integration of Human Structures.* New York: Harper & Row, 1978.

*Rolf, Ida P. "Structural Integration: A Contribution to the Understanding of Stress." *Confinia Psychiatrica* 16 (1973): 69–74.

Rosse, Cornelius, and D. Kay Clawson. *The Musculoskeletal System in Health and Disease.* New York: Harper & Row, 1980.

*Royce, Joseph. *Surface Anatomy.* Philadelphia: Davis, 1965.

Rubin, Lucille S., editor. *Movement for the Actor.* New York: Drama Book Specialists, 1980.

Rywerant, Yochanan. *The Feldenkrais Method: Teaching by Handling.* New York: Giniger, 1983.

Salzer, Felix. *Structural Hearing: Tonal Coherence in Music.* 2 volumes. New York: Dover, 1962.

Samama, Ans. *Muscle Control for Musicians: A Series of Exercises for the Daily Practice.* Utrecht: Bohn, Scheltema and Holkema, 1978.

Satir, Virginia. *Peoplemaking.* Palo Alto, CA: Science and Behavior, 1973.

Schafer, R. Murray. *Ear Cleaning: Notes for an Experimental Music Course.* Don Mills, Ontario, Canada: BMI Canada Limited, 1967.

Schafer, R. Murray. *The Tuning of the World.* New York: Knopf, 1977.

Schenker, Heinrich. *Five Graphic Music Analyses*. New York: Dover, 1969.

*Schenker, Heinrich. *Free Composition*. Edited and translated by Ernst Oster. New York: Longmans, 1979.

*Schilder, Paul. *The Image and Appearance of the Human Body*. New York: International Universities Press, 1950.

*Schwenk, Theodor. *Sensitive Chaos: The Creation of Flowing Forms in Water and Air*. New York: Schocken, 1976.

*Selye, Hans. *The Stress of Life*. New York: McGraw-Hill, 1956.

Selye, Hans. *Stress without Distress*. Philadelphia: Lippincott, 1974.

Shawn, Ted. *Every Little Movement: A Book About François Delsarte*. New York: Dance Horizons, 1963.

Sheldon, William. *Atlas of Men: A Guide for Somatotyping the Adult Male at All Ages*. Darien, CT: Hafner, 1970.

Silverman, Kaja. *The Subject of Semiotics*. New York: Oxford University, 1983.

*Simeon, A. T. W. *Man's Presumptuous Brain*. New York: Dutton, 1962.

Simonton, O. Carl, Stephanie Matthews-Simonton, and J. Creighton. *Getting Well Again: A Step-by-Step, Self-Help Guide to Overcoming Cancer for Patients and Their Families*. Los Angeles: Tarcher, 1978.

Smith, Cyprian. *The Way of Paradox: Spiritual Life as Taught by Meister Eckhart*. New York: Paulist Press, 1987.

*Sobotta, Johannes, and Frank Figge. *Atlas of Human Anatomy*. Baltimore: Urban and Schwarzenberg, 1977.

Spangler, David. *The Laws of Manifestation*. Marina del Rey, CA: DeVorss, 1978.

*Speads, Carola. *Breathing: The ABC's*. New York: Harper & Row, 1978.

Spolin, Viola. *Improvisation for the Theater: A Handbook of Teaching and Directing Techniques*. Evanston: Northwestern University, 1963.

Stanislavski, Constantin. *An Actor Prepares*. Translated by Elizabeth Hapgood. New York: Theatre Arts Books, 1936.

Stanislavski, Constantin. *Building a Character*. New York: Theatre Arts Books, 1949.

Stebbins, Genevieve. *Delsarte System of Expression*. New York: Dance Horizons, 1977.

Stevens, Peter S. *Patterns in Nature*. Boston: Little, Brown, 1974.

Stevens, Wallace. *The Collected Poems of Wallace Stevens*. New York: Knopf, 1957.

Strasberg, Lee. *A Dream of Passion: the Development of the Method*. Boston: Little, Brown, 1987.

Sudnow, David. *Ways of the Hand: The Organization of Improvised Conduct*. Cambridge, MA: Harvard University, 1978.

*Suzuki, Shunryu. *Zen Mind, Beginner's Mind*. New York: Weatherhill, 1970.

*Sweigard, Lulu E. *Human Movement Potential: Its Ideokinetic Facilitation*. New York: Harper & Row, 1974.

Tarasti, Eero. *Myth and Music: A Semiotic Approach to the Aesthetics of Myth in Music, especially that of Wagner, Sibelius and Stravinsky*. Helsinki: Suomen Musiikkitieteellinen Seura, 1978.

Taylor, Harold. *The Pianist's Talent*. New York: Taplinger, 1983.

Teilhard de Chardin, Pierre. *The Phenomenon of Man*. Translated by Bernard Wall. New York: Harper, 1959.

Thomas, Dylan. *The Collected Poems of Dylan Thomas*. New York: New Directions, 1957.

Thoreau, Henry David. *Walden and Other Writings*. Edited by Joseph Wood Krutch. New York: Bantam, 1962. (Originally published 1854.)

Tillich, Paul. *The Courage to Be*. New Haven: Yale University, 1954.

Tillich, Paul. *Dynamics of Faith*. New York: Harper & Row, 1958.

*Tobias, Phillip. *Man, The Tottering Biped: The Evolution of His Posture, Poise and Skill*. Kensington, New South Wales, Australia: Committee in Postgraduate Medical Education, University of New South Wales, 1982.

Todd, Mabel Elsworth. *The Hidden You*. New York: Dance Horizons, 1976. (Originally published 1937.)

*Todd, Mabel Elsworth. *The Thinking Body: A Study of the Balancing Forces of Dynamic Man*. New York: Dance Horizons, 1968.

Trungpa, Chügyam. *Cutting through Spiritual Materialism*. Berkeley: Shambhala, 1973.

Trungpa, Chügyam. "Foundations of Mindfulness." *Garuda IV*. Berkeley, CA: Shambhala, 1976.

Trungpa, Chügyam. *The Myth of Freedom and the Way of Meditation*. Berkeley: Shambhala, 1976.

Tulku, Tarthang. *Gesture of Balance*. Emeryville, CA: Dharma, 1977.

Von Franz, Marie-Louise. *An Introduction to the Interpretation of Fairy Tales*. Dallas: Spring, 1982.

Watts, Alan and Al Chung-liang Huang. *Tao: The Watercourse Way*. New York: Pantheon, 1977.

Wilhelm, Richard, editor and translator. *The I Ching or Book of Changes*. Rendered into English by Cary Baynes. New York: Random House, 1950.

Yeston, Murray, editor. *Readings in Schenker Analysis and Other Approaches*. New Haven: Yale University, 1977.

*Ziegler, Alfred. *Archetypal Medicine*. Dallas: Spring, 1983.

Zuckerkandl, Victor. *Sound and Symbol: Music and the External World*. Translated by Willard Trask. Princeton: Princeton University, 1956.

Index

Movement (*cont.*)
  generous (*cont.*)
      spiritual dimension, 216–217
      touch and, 215–218
    habitual, 109–110, 111
    hierarchical nature, 21–26, 200
    individuality of, 14–15
    phrasing of, 79, 87–88, 167–194
    as self-expression, 80–81
Movement awareness, 86–87; *see also* Percipience
    class, 28–32, 129, 130, 150
    ideal form and, 112–114
Mozart, Wolfgang Amadeus, 22–23, 120
Muscle/musculature, *see also specific muscles*
    abdominal, 56
    of balanced person, 77–78
    body weight and, 39
    function, 39
    hyperactivity, 25
    injured, 162
Muscular contraction: *see* Tension
Music
    body movement and, 23–25
    hierarchical nature of, 22–23, 25
    in reverberative healing, 163, 166
    rhythm and phrase, 79, 176–177

Narcissism, 92
Natural, concept of, 118, 120–121
Naturalness, as generosity, 120–122, 125
Nature, 118, 120
Nervous system, hierarchical arrangement, 24
Neurosis, as arrested development, 120
Noh theater, 183

Olympics, 181, 204
Optometry, 73

Organ chamber, 49, 65
Organs
    abdominal imbalance and, 55–56
    body weight effects, 49, 54–55
Orthotic lifts, 73

Pain, 212–214; *see also* Balance
    in back, 52–53, 84–85
    headache, 103–105
    in lack of core support, 138
    movement education and, 83–85
    reverberative movement and, 161–166
    spasms, 23–25
Paul (the Apostle), 114
Pelvic girdle
    function, 78
    strength mobilization, 128, 129–134
Pelvis
    balance, 45
    imbalance, 51–54
      back pain and, 52–53
      scoliosis-related, 71
Pendency, of body structure, 33–36
Perception, *see also* Percipience
    of body weight, 31–33
    sensory, 100–105
    of time, 126
Percipience, 89–106
    and action, 206–208
    causal thinking and, 105–106
    deftness and, 198–200
    growth of, 216
    human form and, 95–97
    ideals and, 89–91, 108–109
    in reverberative healing, 163
    self-confirmation and, 91–95, 96
    sensory perception, 100–105
    stalking, 97–100
"Performance phrase," 172
Perls, Frederick, 192